Romanticism

A Literary Perspective

Romanticism

A Literary Perspective

F. PARVIN SHARPLESS

HAYDEN BOOK COMPANY, INC.

Rochelle Park, New Jersey

ISBN   0-8104-5069-0
Library of Congress Catalog Card Number   79-50791

1   2   3   4   5   6   7   8   9   PRINTING

79 80 81 82 83 84 85 86 87   YEAR

Preface

The Hayden Humanities Series uses the term "humanities" in both a narrower and broader sense than in many examples of current curriculum structuring. We see humanities texts neither as conglomerations of stuff from literature, art, music, history, and philosophy purporting to express the spirit of a given time or place, nor as collections of readings supposedly illuminating vaguely suggested themes or subjects. Rather, we see them as focusing on the abiding ideas and values that men have wrestled with and lived by, as reflected through literature (broadly defined) and as informed by a variety of man-centered disciplines: psychology, sociology, anthropology, religion, philosophy, history.

The texts in this series deal with the significant human concerns upon which all human actions, great or small, social or individual, are based, whether we know it and admit it or not. These concerns are the stuff of all literature, yesterday and today; and they provide a background for recognizing, understanding, and defining the issues of the moment that claim our attention and wonder.

The approach in these texts is thematic, since such a structure has proved useful in traditional teaching units and in newer elective programs. But again there is a difference. The weakness of the thematic approach has been its tendency to yield units which are impossibly vague or impossibly broad, or both. What we have tried to do is declare and define an idea or issue thoughtfully and deeply so that others may test that declaration and definition through what they read and know, and find dealing with it a cumulative, organic experience, allowing growth and change.

In contrast to most thematically arranged anthologies, these texts do not pretend a faceless editor or the illusion of authorial objectivity or distance. The compiler has a voice and a point of view, and a conviction that he knows what he is talking about. The introductory essay both introduces and interprets; it defines an idea or issue—in this case *Romanticism*—and then tries to see it in the round by explaining its past, asserting its continuing vitality and viability, and suggesting some of the things that can be done with it.

This approach takes us far beyond the usual "knowing about" or "talking about" to which literature is too often reduced. We believe the themes have lasting value as organizing constructs for making sense out of our world and for comprehending how the literary artist makes sense out of it. The themes also have a coherence that such thematic structures as, say, "Man and Society" or "Man and the Environment" or "War and Peace" cannot possibly have. One import of both these observations is that the question of "modern" literature vs. "classical" or "traditional" makes little real sense. Literature, by our lights, is always new and renewable. Forever is now. The idiom and the cultural demands and expectations may be different, but the underlying human concerns that the artist is examining are timeless and universal—and that's what counts.

The reader is not expected to agree with everything in the introduction, but is urged to consider it carefully; a casual reading won't do. The argument needs to be understood, and then questions must be raised about validity, emphasis, application, ramification, relevance to experience, and ultimate usefulness in ordering ideas, feelings, beliefs and values. The defining essay should be a point of departure and a point of return. Along with the headnotes and questions for each group of selections, it serves as a guide for analysis and discussion, not as a gospel to be ingested, remembered, and regurgitated.

There is no attempt in these texts at coverage of literary periods or schools of writing, but there is a variety of genres, modes, backgrounds, times, and writers. Certain long works have been excerpted; enough has been included from any work to feed the thematic demands and yet not misrepresent the total piece. The aim throughout has been to show how widely diffused in our literature the central concern of each text has been and still is. In the final section, suggestions are made for reading full novels and plays that could not be included in a text of this size.

Romanticism: A Literary Perspective is a generalist's book, which attempts to simplify and put into more common use a few complex and significant ideas. It is intended therefore for generalists —both students and teachers—who find education more useful when it offers large ideas with some evidence and context than when it offers small ideas with copious documentation.

There are, of course, more specialized approaches to these topics through anthropology, linguistics, psychology, religion, and history, as well as traditional literary study. But some ideas are too central to liberal and humane learning to be left exclusively to the scholars, and if we wait until we are fully wise enough, it might be too late.

F. PARVIN SHARPLESS
Series Editor

Contents

Romanticism

A Literary Perspective

Introduction

It is the fundamental argument of historians of the Romantic Movement (and of this volume) that in the decades at the end of the 18th and the beginning of the 19th centuries a basic change occurred in the consciousness of Western culture. The radical character of this change was recognized by the poets and artists of that time, and the ideas and emotions this consciousness produced can be traced in their works. However, because Romanticism represents a major change in the way people think about the fundamental assumptions of their lives, its effects reach beyond those particular few artists and forward in time. These changes continue, their effects multiply, until today their currency is everywhere, embedded in modern values and institutions, affecting the lives of people who have never heard of Romanticism or thought of themselves as Romantic. Indeed, it can be argued that the last few decades in America have witnessed the establishment of Romantic thought as a major influence and style: that on fundamental questions of life, on religious, moral, and political questions, on matters of taste, both popular and refined, on questions of metaphysics and cosmology, Romanticism is in the ascendancy.

If this is so, it seems clear that we would be in a better position to understand the temper and character of modern life if we understood better its philosophic assumptions and the historical unfolding of the Romantic Movement and attitudes. To learn where we are, to see the development of attitudes, ideas, and values in terms of the past, to see today as a result of the historical forces with which we live, is to gain new, liberating perspectives. To this end, this volume offers students the chance to study as an academic problem the intellectual and emotional processes set forth in the literature of Romanticism. It allows them to review the premises of the early 19th century views that prevailed in the fields of psychology, religion, and politics and to think through, from poem to poem, from document to document, the intellectual and psychological states and events described there.

To do this profitably, one need not agree with or accept Romantic attitudes, although it is difficult to escape from their influence. Most readers will have little difficulty recognizing familiar questions on which they already have some opinion. Assumptions contrary to Romanticism existed prior to and during the rise of Romantic consciousness, and these contraries continue to exist. Indeed, it is clear that the traditional judgments of things, the traditional values against which Romanticism in some of its forms was a rebellion, still exist, often in forms similar to 18th century Classicism itself, which was based on the Judeo-Christian tradition that pervaded Western culture for 500 to 600 years before 1800. These provide a complement, sometimes a polar opposite, and knowledge of one helps to define and understand the other, whichever an individual may find personally more sympathetic. This volume does simplify the two points of view and separate them as opposites, but it is clear that both of them remain modern and vital, both contribute to the way people continue to live and think about the serious aspects of their lives.

Romanticism and Classicism

The difference between these two positions is fundamental and easy to illustrate. In the traditional or Classical view, authority for truth, for power, for social or moral value was derived from a hierarchical view of human existence. The primary figure for these relationships was that of a great chain that connected the highest levels of existence to the lower, from God at the top downward to human beings and onward to animal and mineral forms of matter. Correct behavior, one's function, morality, and relationships were determined by the place in this chain. Thus, one's religious duties and obligations were created by one's relation to God, one's political duties by relation to the king and the nobility. At home, one acquired power or accepted subservience by whether one was the parent or the child, the older or the younger. In none of these systems was there much mobility: Providence, or God's Will, or Birth, placed one into a Place, and one's duty, one's sense of the purposes of life was created by that Place. To accept or submit to that definition was to be happy; to rebel, to want more, to doubt divine or political authority was wrong and certain to cause unhappiness to oneself and others.

Such a view is, of course, conservative and, as long as most people accept it, stable. It does not encourage Change, or Aspiration, or Bettering Oneself, or Rising in the World. It does not encourage doing better than one's parents, or believing that the world could be better, or even wishing that it were. It says, in short, that things are the way they are. Fates and ordinances, natural and divine, surround one's life and limit it. To fight against these restraints, to wish to be higher or better or richer or different, is to make oneself unhappy. Since parents and the King and God know best, harmony and tranquility, both for the individual and society, are best achieved by the child's or subject's firm acceptance of that principle. (The essential argument for this position is given in Section I, in Pope's *Essay on Man*.)

Romanticism expresses an opposite notion: It holds that one can determine for oneself answers to social, political, and religious questions, that one has rights and opportunities inherent in his or her particular case, that being an individual, one has individual needs that one should strive to fulfill. To the Romantic, Ambition, Imagination, and Self-Determination are virtues, and the proper course of life is to work and struggle to attain these goals—that is, to attempt Self-Fulfillment. Essential to these ends is Freedom: freedom for an individual to choose how to live, where to live, what values and social codes to accept, and what to reject. To the Romantic, a person comes into the world "unsponsored," alone, with an Adam-like innocence and childish blankness of potential upon which the Will or the Soul or the Self writes, out of which personality is made. Life is the action of this Self—the Process of its Realization.

The traditional or Classical view is that human nature is such that, without outside definitions and limits, it will become destructive and evil to itself and to society. The restraints of social and moral authority, indeed, are necessary in order for any freedom to exist. One must be bound in order to move; law and order provide the basis of any coherent view of life. To the Romantic, put simply, restraints are tyrannical and threatening. They impose stifling limits on the personality and its inherent need to express itself without restraint. Rebellion is a central Romantic attitude; the Self is forged in the heat of its encounters with the social and moral restraints of the Establishment. As the child throws off the values and beliefs of the parents in order to become a self, so Romantic writers must define their Personality against the efforts of the Tradition to enslave them by holding them to existing patterns of allowable experience.

Put in contemporary terms, it is clear that many of our social, political, and moral decisions are determined by whether we accept traditional patterns of behavior, doing what our parents have told us to do, accepting the codes of conduct that are "given," or whether we question those points of view, asking our own questions, acting on our own judgments of right and wrong, determining answers to these questions out of our own experience. *Doesn't reason dictate this?* Should one accept God's Providence as absolute, or should one raise questions about that authority? Should one follow conscience against the social norm? Should one reject the life style of the majority if one hears a different drummer?

These distinctions are, of course, not as absolute as this discussion may suggest. We all make choices in varying degrees between these extremes, and our choices depend on the particular issue, on our state of mind at the time, on our age, and on many other factors. More realistically, we should ask where and when we should take one view and where the other? To what extent and when should our lives be formed in conformity to traditional values and ideas, sanctioned by history and codified by law? To what extent and when can we make up our own sense of reality, define our acts in terms of our individual needs, see the purpose of life to be an effort to fulfill these personal ambitions?

We do make choices. Most of our daily actions, both serious and light, momentous and trivial, occur on the basis of one set or the other of assumptions about personality and values. This book is aimed at making readers more conscious of the philosophic assumptions of these differences, at making them more aware of the modern or Romantic points of view, and at bringing them to see the important markers along the pathway of intellectual history that have produced these conditions, attitudes, and states of mind we call Romantic. Although some of the ideas and some of the works included are in the language and idiom of a past time, the philosophic problems and the arguments and feelings about them continue. Indeed, some of the problems have become commonplace and familiar. Therefore, we need to know about them and their history and to make our own judgments about them.

PART I

Your Romanticist-Classicist Quotient

Your Romanticist-Classicist Quotient (R-C Q): A Test

The selections in this volume will affect readers in different ways. If, however, as has been argued, Romanticism is a distinctively new conception and if its content has affected modern consciousness, we should all have points of sympathy with major aspects of these works. Yet human beings are complicated. They change their styles and their minds, and even the simplest person is more complex than most ideas and more complex than most of our ideas about people. Thus, in a basic sense we are all combinations, logical and otherwise, of opposing conceptions—some Romantic, some Classical, and some mixtures of the two.

The following "test" is a device to help you think about ways in which Romantic and Classical attitudes do indeed reveal themselves in everyday life. It may help both to clarify the issues and ideas themselves and to see connections between them and daily matters of style and judgment. There is, of course, no "right" answer, any more than Romanticism or Classicism can be seen as offering the entire truth on any given question or style. The questions are not scientific. They should be given subjective responses, and the answers chosen should be those closest to what you think. When the test is finished, score the responses by means of the table of scores and explanations. Make only one choice for each question.

QUESTIONS

1. When things go wrong and you feel angry and confused, what do you customarily conclude?
   a. It's probably my fault.
   b. Someone up there doesn't like me.
   c. I'll have to do better next time.
   d. Damn the Fates!
   e. Why don't those stupid so-and-so's get things straightened out?
   f. So it goes.

2. What kind of learning-classroom situation do you find most congenial?
   a. A clear, logical tight structure of lectures from which one can record clear, exact notes.
   b. A great deal of discussion and sharing of ideas and feelings.
   c. A teacher who sets high standards and insists that students meet them.

d. A teacher who springs surprises and interesting new ideas.

e. A teacher who hands out a detailed syllabus on the first day of class and follows it to the letter.

f. A class in which the teacher stays in the background allowing students to meet the material directly.

3. Which of the following statements do you find most acceptable?

a. The lower classes need our help to improve themselves.

b. People are people whatever their background.

c. Very few people successfully overcome a poor background.

d. You meet interesting people on trolley cars.

e. One should choose one's friends from one's own social class.

f. Poor people are nice to visit, but I wouldn't want to live with one.

g. Higher capacities of the human spirit are always able to overcome economic or educational deficiencies.

4. Which of the following statements do you find most acceptable?

a. Sex is a means by which one can overcome alienation and self-consciousness.

b. Sex is overrated.

c. Sex is fun.

d. Sex is funny.

e. Sex is dangerous.

f. Sex is biological.

g. Sexual attraction is a healthy dialectic between male and female.

h. Sexual union with the right person can be a high achievement of the human spirit.

i. Sex is a means of expressing the deeper powers of the spirit.

j. Relations between the sexes is one of the more interesting games people play.

5. In your nightmares how do you imagine Hell (or, if you imagine Hell, how is it)?

a. A tropical jungle thick with vines and creepers.

b. A small room filled with people talking closely and intensely.

c. A frozen tundra stretching to the horizon.

d. A pit full of mud.

e. A balloon drifting higher into the blue sky.

f. A sandy desert.

6. At this moment the condition of your bureau, dressing table, or desk is:

a. Top neat, drawers tidy.

b. Top neat, drawers untidy.

c. Drawers tidy, top cluttered.

d. Drawers untidy, top cluttered.

7. If someone gave you $500 and required you to spend it all at once, which of the following would you spend it on?
   a. An expensive antique pot.
   b. A night of dinner, theater, and nightclubs.
   c. A set of Sierra Club photographs.
   d. An autographed letter by T.S. Eliot.
   e. A day at the racetrack.
   f. A new living room rug.
   g. A grove of fruit trees for the birds to sing in.
   h. A fence around your house.
   i. A gift for your parents.

8. Guilt is:
   a. Useful to correct and improve human conduct.
   b. A necessary deterrent to socially unacceptable actions by individuals.
   c. Part of a slave mentality.
   d. Depressing.
   e. A psychological weapon used by parents and other authorities to limit the freedom and self-expression of children.
   f. A condition common to humanity, and of little concern.
   g. Something to be overcome by good works.
   h. What people deserve for their disobedience.

9. Space travel is:
   a. A supreme fulfillment of man's destiny.
   b. A triumph of beautiful technology, accurate and precise.
   c. An amusing but idle entertainment.
   d. An escape from genuine problems on earth.
   e. A foolish flight to sterility and nothingness.
   f. A search for God in the right place.
   g. A search for God in the wrong place.

10. History is:
    a. A record of the decline of Western civilization.
    b. A record of progress, achievement, and developing consciousness.
    c. A record of symbolic and mythical modes of expression.
    d. A scientific collection of factual data about the past.
    e. The return to consciousness of repressed materials.
    f. Relative to the age in which it is written.
    g. Bunk.
    h. A collection of useful lessons without knowledge of which we are doomed to repeat history's mistakes.

i. A collection of instructive examples showing the dangers of egotism and rebellion.

11. The primary impulse leading a painter to paint an attractive nude is:
    a. A tribute to his/her mistress's/lover's beauty or handsomeness.
    b. An interest in curves, angles, planes, and color textures.
    c. The desire to incorporate beauty in a work of art.
    d. Erotic and libidinous.
    e. An expression of emotion to be discarded when finished.

12. The best poetry is that which:
    a. Imitates or describes the external world of nature.
    b. Follows the forms that tradition dictates.
    c. Influences the reader to become a better person by describing models of excellence.
    d. Expresses most fully the soul of the poet.
    e. Contains the clearest structure.
    f. Contains a spontaneous overflow of powerful feelings.
    g. Has oft been said, but ne'er so well expressed.

13. Your favorite composer from the following list is:
    a. Brahms
    b. Sibelius
    c. Tchaikowsky
    d. Wagner
    e. Bach
    f. Mahler
    g. Haydn
    h. Mozart
    i. Telemann
    j. Richard Strauss

14. Your favorite painter from the following list is:
    a. Turner
    b. Renoir
    c. Mondrian
    d. Reynolds
    e. Gainsborough
    f. Constable

15. What is your favorite season?
    a. Spring
    b. Summer
    c. Fall
    d. Winter

16. If you were to live in another country, what would be your choice?
    a. India
    b. Canada
    c. Italy
    d. Sweden
    e. Scotland
    f. Jamaica

17. Your favorite spectator sport from the following list is:
    a. Football
    b. Baseball
    c. Ice hockey
    d. Gymnastics or diving

18. Male version: The most admirable kind of woman is one who:
    a. Is a good cook.
    b. Is quiet, modest, and unassuming.
    c. Sometimes swears and tells risqué jokes.
    d. Is a nurse or secretary.
    e. Can sometimes win at poker.
    f. Can adjust a carburetor.
    g. Wears her hair long and little disheveled.
    h. Is a cute gal who can be a pal.

19. Female version: The most admirable kind of man is one who:
    a. Is robust, athletic, and manly.
    b. Writes poetry.
    c. Sings sweet love songs.
    d. Knows how much to tip the waiter.
    e. Takes charge.
    f. Has very good manners.
    g. Is not afraid to show how he feels.
    h. Is small, wiry, and intense.

20. Nature is:
    a. Beautifully designed.
    b. Full of raw energy.
    c. Nice in the garden.
    d. Nice in the woods and forests.

Romanticist-Classicist Quotient: Key to Scoring

Answers are scored on a basis of a range from zero to 10, with 10 representing an extreme Romantic position, zero being an extreme Classical position. (If the reader wishes, he or she may reverse the scale, making the scores opposite, giving Classicism the higher number and Romanticism the lower.) If all answers are Romantic, a score of 200 will be produced. If all answers are Classical, the score will be zero. Before you begin, ask yourself whether you'd prefer being known as a Romantic or a Classicist.

Question 1: a=0, b=2, c=3, d=8, e=10, f=5

This question considers the relation of the individual to the universe and defines the importance or value of the Self. The Romantic view that the Self's perceptions determine what is real is opposite to the Classicist view that what is real exists as an absolute, permanent entity apart from an individual's perception of it. The Romantic hero is often seen making defiant gestures at the sky where the tyrannical sky gods live aloof in majesty and power. However, the Classicist deference to form and to the social and religious embodiments of form requires the belief that if things go wrong it is human agency that is at fault, individual responsibility that has been shirked and should be acknowledged.

Question 2: a=0, b=8, c=2, d=7, e=1, f=10

Relation to authority is the issue here as well as the degree of external form one requires. Organic form, the idea that the style of doing something is derived from the specific circumstances of the individual case, is a Romantic notion. Thus, a course or class that evolves according to spontaneous emotions and currents of thought is a Romantic experience, and a teacher who designs or encourages or allows such procedure is a Romantic teacher. The opposite situation is a teacher who feels that he or she is responsible for the absolute, permanent form of the material, that it can be presented in only one way, and that deviations from that form are harmful and dissident. Because Classicists are more authority-conscious, they will be more likely to feel responsible for the decorum and standards in the classroom and will be more likely to assume the role of the prescriber of value. In extreme cases, they may become the course themselves, although there are Romantic teachers whose ego rather than their interest in enforcing the discipline they teach may become the center of everyone's attention. If the teacher's authority is used to stimulate and push and encourage students to their own originality and stimulation, it is a Romantic situation. If the teacher's authority is used to enforce a single view of the material and to insist on the strict proprieties of its learning and repetition, the situation is Classical. Classical views of learning emphasize tradition and imitation. They hold that the past embodies truths — common, normal, natural — and that the best test of the truth is the test of time. Therefore, what has been known and respected over long periods of time is most likely to be true. New ideas and originality itself are to be mistrusted.

Question 3: a=2, b=8, c=0, d=10, e=2, f=1, g=9

Democracy and social mobility are revolutionary ideas and are associated with the sense that an individual can make of herself whatever her capacities and inherent strengths will support. The definition of a person in a social context, on the other hand, is a Classical notion. A person's place means "knowing" that place in social terms: gentleman, aristocrat, worker, or merchant; bachelor, husband, wife, or mistress. In the Classical novels of Jane Austen or Henry James, the determinants of behavior are social. (In *Wuthering Heights*, a Romantic novel, Heathcliffe and Cathy defy society.) People decide in Classical works what they want on the basis of social values. A good Classical society, according to this view, is not democratic but contains relationships based on acceptance of difference and the notion that higher, more privileged members of the social body have a paternalistic concern for others. This view implies a notion of "breeding" or "cultivation," which some people have and others lack, and which education of "getting ahead" cannot overcome. The Classical society is, of course, the more conservative politically, although some extreme Romantic forms of society are also antidemocratic when they rely on a special leader or hero.

Question 4: a=8, b=2, c=9, d=3, e=0, f=2, g=8, h=10, i=8, j=2

Because sexual energies are unstable, dynamic, and powerful, the Classical view is that they are dangerous, causing unhappiness, discord, and misery, and dangerous also to the stability of society unless they are controlled by social usage and convention. The Classical view also takes a comic line about sexuality: The comedy of manners or sexual farce treats sex as a joke, thus making it more socialized and less dangerous. The Romantic view takes sexuality seriously. The very energy and vitality of sex are important parts of one's individuality, and much of the individual's self-expression is of a sexual character. To some Romantics, sexuality offers a means by which the isolation of the Self can be overcome through the power of Eros, which connects the otherwise isolated Self with the Other, or which creates a basis for interdependency, either between a pair of lovers or between the individual and life outside the Self, other people, or other organic forces. Whitman is most outspoken in declaring the sexual basis of human love. Eliot, on the other hand, is most distressed by the vulgarity of sexual appetites, unpurified by spiritual qualities.

Question 5: a=0, b=0, c=10, d=0, e=8, f=10

This question suggests typical Romantic and Classical imagery and scenery (see also Question 17). The basic question is whether one fears isolation or proximity. The Romantic, of course, fears isolation. Being already subjective, he requires connections with others and fears being "alone, alone on a wide wide sea," or a desert, or other sterile, empty, uninhabited place. The Classicist, on the other hand, likes to keep his distance, likes to have connections governed by conventions; he fears immersion, drowning, being in crowds, jungles, cities, drawing rooms, places where organic processes of growth and sexual energies are pressing in upon him. Consider Conrad's Marlow keeping to the middle of the river, out of the jungle, as he investigates the Heart of Darkness.

Question 6: a=3, b=0, c=10, d=7

This question concerns inner and outer forms. Romantic ideas of form suggest that the inner basic structures of the matter are more important than the particular aspects of the appearance. Classical ideas suggest that the external form is more important and indicates a comformity to traditional behavior. If you are entirely tidy or entirely messy, you lack seriousness about the problem.

Question 7: a=1, b=9, c=0, d=1, e=9, f=1, g=10, h=2, i=2

The distinction here is between experience and things, between events occurring in time and therefore having an end, and things that are permanent, that one can keep and care for indefinitely. Antique things also suggest permanence and the ability of artifacts or works to exist in the face of change.

Question 8: a=1, b=1, c=8, d=7, e=10, f=7, g=1, h=0

Guilt is a condition of self-doubt, of negation. If it is felt to be deserved, it also implies a poor sense of the worth of human personality and freedom. Where it is institutionalized, in some churches or in totalitarian ideologies, and sometimes in families, it may destroy individuality and the desire for revolution on the part of parishioners or children. When human nature is seen as fallen into sin or disobedience to law, then guilt is seen as appropriate punishment for the transgression. Where there is no external law, as in a Romantic point of view, then there is less of an external standard to fall from, and therefore less guilt. But a person with no sense of guilt is capable of anything.

Question 9: a=0, b=3, c=7, d=8, e=10, f=1, g=9

This question also reflects on the imagery of Romantic and Classical literature. Romantic thought contains more inner, lower, darker places: caves, dark tunnels, jungles. Classical thought aspires to higher and purer conditions than the earthly and human; therefore, it admires the sky and places its Divinities in the heavens. The image of a human being, sterilized, encased in a grotesque space suit, locked in an artificial atmosphere, surrounded by mathematical machines, and then soaring into the sky where there is no art and no life is, in the Romantic view, a futile and inhuman business. Classicism, on the other hand, admires aspiration, especially upward toward God and Goodness, and also takes much joy in the wonders of science. A similar exaltation is sought by the mountain climber, who craves to climb the mountain because "it's there." There is Romantic aspiration, of course (see Barth's *Night-Sea Journey*), but it is carried out by individuals, and the pains are more spiritual and less physical. Robert Frost's "Birches" talks about the need for balance in climbing. For further discussion see "The Structure of Modern Mythology" in *Symbol and Myth in Modern Literature* (Hayden, 1976).

Question 10: a=2, b=8, c=10, d=2, e=9, f=7, g=4, h=1, i=0

Classical views suggest that the old days were the best days, that progress is unlikely, that change is decline. Romanticism, more interested in the interior consciousness than in exterior fact, is therefore more interested in mythology and in symbolic discourse than in narrowly conceived historical data. The Romantic, aware of change and evolution, sees that each age has a view of itself that succeeding ages amend to suit themselves. Traditionalists consider that history teaches lessons, usually cautionary and conservative ones, about the follies of human endeavor and the high price of ambition.

Question 11: a=8, b=0, c=1, d=8, e=10

Classical art emphasizes the form and the general aspects of human experience. Romantic art emphasizes the particular and the individual and is more interested in the content than the form. Thus, an interest in the particular lady or gentleman's charms is Romantic, any interest in generic charm is Classical. A static interest in Beauty is Classical, and kinetic interest in the physical is Romantic.

Question 12: a=0, b=0, c=2, d=9, e=2, f=10, g=0

Form, imitation of traditional forms, ornamentation of received values are Classical; personal, spontaneous self-expression is Romantic.

Question 13: a=6, b=8, c=8, d=10, e=3, f=10, g=0, h=2, i=1, j=10

Question 14: a=8, b=10, c=0, d=1, e=2, f=5

These assignments are perhaps arbitrary, and the reader may amend them as he wishes. Painting and music in which form predominates over content is Classical, as in poetry. Romantic painting is often about common people or street scenes or about large dramatic moments. Classical painting is about lines and colors or upper-class subjects in their gardens and drawing rooms. Romantic music often has a "program" (the *1812 Overture, Daphnis and Chloe*). Classical music emphasizes cadences and harmony. Romantic music begins when Christian liturgy loses its place as the central subject of music, as in the Mass.

Question 15: a=0, b=5, c=10, d=2

This question turns on the degree to which Nature and energy are held in bounds by seasons, just as, in another way, one's choice of scenery depends on the degree to which nature and energy are formed by latitude or climatic conditions. Spring is a time of modest growth, although to some Classicists it too is too strong, the cruelest months. The Romantic likes ripeness and thus Fall is the best time, the time of fruition, fulfillment, and a touch of nostalgic melancholy and decline. See Keats's "To Autumn."

Question 16: a=8, b=2, c=10, d=2, e=0, f=8

Rocks, mountains, spare trees, and shrubs, the scoured straight outlines of rockbound coasts, Norwegian pines with their pale somber greens and grays are Classical. Maine is Classical; the Florida swamps are Romantic. A whole generation of American writers thought that England and New England were Nordic and social and structured and that Italy was the place of decadence, a symbol of license or of gaiety and a freer life. See Hawthorne and James. The Sierra Club photographs are eminently Classical, emphasizing contorted limbs of dead trees, deserts with timid wildflowers, rocks in fantastic shapes, and rarely showing any living soul—animal or human. Compare the collections of photographs called *The Family of Man* in which we see people in all manner of humble conditions of life. Compare also the abstract painter with Renoir and Renoir's interest in common life and common people in the flesh.

Question 17: a=0, b=10, c=0, d=10

To understand the values in Question 17 one must note the existence of Game Reversal Theory, which says that in a game all values of life are reversed. Thus, a Romantic likes Classical games, and vice versa because they are games, not real life. Thus, a Romantic likes baseball because it is the most stylized, the most formal, the most traditional, the most out-of-time game. The Romantic would not tolerate the slow pace, the attention to ritual, and the accumulation of minutiae if it were real. Similarly, the violent emotions of the spectator at a football or hockey game would threaten the Classicist if it was not contained within the rules of the game and within the confines of the stadium or rink. Football is a Romantic game for the players because it is played on the face of the earth and is mostly a muddle except when a brilliant effort creates order from chaos for a moment. Gymnastics and diving are, of course, like dance, very formal and require discipline and attention to detail.

Question 18 (Male): a=0, b=1, c=9, d=2, e=9, f=10, g=10, h=0

Question 19 (Female): a=1, b=7, c=8, d=0, e=0, f=2, g=10, h=10

These answers suggest control of emotional and sexual energy by formal convention. Thus, the Classicist prefers "roles" that are conventional and sexually typed, so that sexual energy is not freed for the individual to feel. The Romantic likes dialectical relations, sexual as much as any, and therefore likes sexual roles that emphasize sexual difference. Romantic dress and style are more ostentatiously sexual in character; Classical dress and style may be pretty, or hint at erotic matters, but must do so discreetly.

Question 20: a=0, b=10, c=2, d=8

As in scenery, the energies are controlled or not.

PART II

Classicism and Romanticism:
The Basic Positions

Classicism and Romanticism: The Basic Positions

There is no simple account of the fundamental ideas of classicism. The idea has a long history and has had many brilliant statements, some hopeful, some grim, some defiant, some humble. This section of Pope's poem is one of the most striking and most interesting of these statements of the traditional view because Pope is not arguing simply that authority must be accepted on faith or that history and stability require it. His view is that a reasonable person, one who has achieved a measure of good sense and a realistic view of the world, will come to the same conclusions as one who proceeds by faith in traditional values asserted by traditional authorities. Thus, it is possible, in Pope's view, to think for oneself *and* be a traditionalist. His argument is made with good humor. By its logical plan, its clarity, and its copious citations of illustrations and examples, it makes its appeal to rational intelligence.

Thus, as we read we can concentrate on the point of view given: a cool, elegant, exact, and absolute statement of the superiority of God's manifest providence, revealed to human beings by means of Human Reason, and illustrated by the Designs of Nature. It is this position from which Romantic dissent begins.

ESSAY ON MAN (BOOK I)

Alexander Pope (1688–1744)

> Awake, my St. John!° leave all meaner things
> To low ambition, and the pride of kings.
> Let us (since life can little more supply
> Than just to look about us and to die)
> Expatiate° free o'er all this scene of man;   5
> A mighty maze! but not without a plan;
> A wild, where weeds and flowers promiscuous shoot;
> Or garden, tempting with forbidden fruit.
> Together let us beat° this ample field,
> Try what the open, what the covert yield;   10
> The latent tracts, the giddy heights explore
> Of all who blindly creep, or sightless soar;
> Eye Nature's walks, shoot folly as it flies,
> And catch the manners living as they rise;

°*St. John:*   Henry St. John, Viscount Bolingbroke, Pope's philosophical teacher and patron   °*Expatiate:*   enlarge upon   °*beat:*   explore

Laugh where we must, be candid where we can;   15
But vindicate the ways of God to man.

I

Say first, of God above, or man below,
What can we reason, but from what we know?
Of man, what see we but his station here,
From which to reason, or to which refer?   20
Through worlds unnumbered though the God be known,
'Tis ours to trace him only in our own.
He, who through vast immensity can pierce,
See worlds on worlds compose one universe,
Observe how system into system runs,   25
What other planets circle other suns,
What varied being peoples every star,
May tell why Heaven has made us as we are.
But of this frame the bearings, and the ties,
The strong connections, nice° dependencies,   30
Gradations just, has thy pervading soul
Looked through? or can a part contain the whole?
    Is the great chain, that draws all to agree,
And drawn supports, upheld by God, or thee?

II

Presumptuous man! the reason wouldst thou find,   35
Why formed so weak, so little, and so blind?
First, if thou canst, the harder reason guess,
Why formed no weaker, blinder, and no less?
Ask of thy mother earth, why oaks are made
Taller and stronger than the weeds they shade?   40
Or ask of yonder argent fields above,
Why Jove's satellites are less than Jove?
    Of systems possible, if 'tis confessed
That wisdom infinite must form the best,
Where all must fall or not coherent be,   45
And all that rises, rise in due degree;
Then, in the scale of reasoning life, 'tis plain,
There must be, somewhere, such a rank as man:
And all the question (wrangle e'er so long)
Is only this, if God has placed him wrong?   50

°*nice:* exact

Respecting man, whatever wrong we call,
May, must be right, as relative to all.
In human works, though labored on with pain,
A thousand movements scarce one purpose gain;
In God's, one single can its end produce;   55
Yet serves to second too some other use.
So man, who here seems principal alone,
Perhaps acts second to some sphere unknown,
Touches some wheel, or verges to some goal;
'Tis but a part we see, and not a whole.   60
    When the proud steed shall know why man restrains
His fiery course, or drives him o'er the plains;
When the dull ox, why now he breaks the clod,
Is now a victim, and now Egypt's god:
Then shall man's pride and dullness comprehend   65
His actions', passions', being's, use and end;
Why doing, suffering, checked, impelled; and why
This hour a slave, the next a deity.
    Then say not man's imperfect, Heaven in fault;
Say rather, man's as perfect as he ought: 70
His knowledge measured to his state and place;
His time a moment, and a point his space.
If to be perfect in a certain sphere,
What matter, soon or late, or here or there?
The blest today is as completely so,   75
As who began a thousand years ago.

III

Heaven from all creatures hides the book of fate,
All but the page prescribed, their present state:
From brutes what men, from men what spirits know:°
Or who could suffer being here below?   80
The lamb thy riot dooms to bleed today,
Had he thy reason, would he skip and play?
Pleased to the last, he crops the flowery food,
And licks the hand just raised to shed his blood.
Oh blindness to the future! kindly given.   85
That each may fill the circle marked by Heaven:
Who sees with equal eye, as God of all,
A hero perish, or a sparrow fall,
Atoms or systems into ruin hurled,
And now a bubble burst, and now a world.   90

°*From brutes . . . spirits know:*   Heaven hides from brutes what men know.

Hope humbly then; with trembling pinions° soar;
Wait the great teacher death; and God adore.
What future bliss, He gives not thee to know,
But gives that hope to be thy blessing now.
Hope springs eternal in the human breast: 95
Man never is, but always to be blest:
The soul, uneasy and confined from home,
Rests and expatiates in a life to come.
    Lo, the poor Indian! whose untutored mind
Sees God in clouds, or hears Him in the wind;   100
His soul, proud science never taught to stray
Far as the solar-walk, or milky way;
Yet simple Nature to his hope has given,
Behind the cloud-topped hill, an humbler heaven;
Some safer world in depth of woods embraced,   105
Some happier island in the watery waste,
Where slaves once more their native land behold,
No fiends torment, no Christians thirst for gold.
To be, contents his natural desire,
He asks no angel's wings, no seraph's fire;   110
But thinks, admitted to that equal sky,
His faithful dog shall bear him company.

                                    IV

Go, wiser thou! and in thy scale of sense,
Weigh thy opinion against Providence;
Call imperfection what thou fanciest such,   115
Say, here He gives too little, there too much:
Destroy all creatures for thy sport or gust,°
Yet cry, If man's unhappy, God's unjust;
If man alone engross not Heaven's high care,
Alone made perfect here, immortal there: 120
Snatch from his hand the balance and the rod,
Rejudge his justice, be the God of God.
In pride, in reasoning pride, our error lies;
All quit their sphere, and rush into the skies.
Pride still is aiming at the blessed abodes,   125
Men would be angels, angels would be gods.
Aspiring to be gods, if angels fell,
Aspiring to be angels, men rebel:

°*pinions:* wings; that is, aspire modestly, fly upward with deference   °*gust:* taste,
appetite

And who but wishes to invert the laws
Of order, sins against th' Eternal Cause.   130

v

Ask for what end the heavenly bodies shine,
Earth for whose use? Pride answers, " 'Tis for mine:
For me kind Nature wakes her genial power,
Suckles each herb, and spreads out every flower;
Annual for me, the grape, the rose renew,   135
The juice nectareous, and the balmy dew;
For me, the mine a thousand treasures brings;
For me, health gushes from a thousand springs;
Seas roll to waft me, suns to light me rise;
My footstool earth, my canopy the skies."   140
   But errs not Nature from this gracious end,
From burning suns° when livid deaths descend,
When earthquakes swallow, or when tempests sweep
Towns to one grave, whole nations to the deep?
"No" ('tis replied) "the first Almighty Cause   145
Acts not by partial, but by general laws;
Th' exceptions few; some change since all began:
And what created perfect?"—Why then man?
If the great end be human happiness,
Then Nature deviates; and can man do less?   150
As much that end a constant course requires
Of showers and sunshine, as of man's desires;
As much eternal springs and cloudless skies,
As men forever temperate, calm, and wise.
If plagues or earthquakes break not Heaven's design,   155
Why then a Borgia,° or a Catiline?°
Who knows but He, whose hand the lightning forms,
Who heaves old ocean, and who wings the storms;
Pours fierce ambition in a Caesar's mind,
Or turns young Ammon° loose to scourge mankind?   160
From pride, from pride, our very reasoning springs;
Account for moral as for natural things:
Why charge we Heaven in those, in these acquit?
In both, to reason right is to submit.
   Better for us, perhaps, it might appear,   165
Were there all harmony, all virtue here;

°*burning suns:* Plagues and illness occur in summer.   °*Borgia:* Cesare Borgia
(1476–1507)   °*Catiline:* Roman conspirator denounced by Cicero.
°*Ammon:* Alexander the Great

That never air or ocean felt the wind;
That never passion discomposed the mind.
But all subsists by elemental strife;
And passions are the elements of life.   170
The general order, since the whole began,
Is kept by Nature, and is kept in man.

VI

What would this man? Now upward will he soar,
And little less than angel, would be more;
Now looking downwards, just as grieved appears,   175
To want the strength of bulls, the fur of bears.
Made for his use all creatures if he call,
Say what their use, had he the powers of all?
Nature to these,° without profusion, kind,
The proper organs, proper powers assigned;   180
Each seeming want° compensated of course,
Here with degrees of swiftness, there of force;
All in exact proportion to the state;
Nothing to add, and nothing to abate.
Each beast, each insect, happy in its own: 185
Is Heaven unkind to man, and man alone?
Shall he alone, whom rational we call,
Be pleased with nothing, if not blessed with all?
    The bliss of man (could pride that blessing find)
Is not to act or think beyond mankind;   190
No powers of body or of soul to share,
But what his nature and his state can bear.
Why has not man a microscopic eye?
For this plain reason, man is not a fly.°
Say what the use, were finer optics given,   195
To inspect a mite, not comprehend the heaven?
Or touch, if tremblingly alive all o'er,
To smart and agonize at every pore?
Or quick effluvia° darting through the brain,
Die of a rose in aromatic pain?   200
If Nature thundered in his opening ears,
And stunned him with the music of the spheres,
How would he wish that Heaven had left him still
The whispering zephyr, and the purling rill?

°*these:* animals   °*want:* deficiency   °*not a fly:* Flies were believed to have
microscopic vision.   °*effluvia:* particles thought to convey odors

Who finds not Providence all good and wise,   205
Alike in what it gives, and what denies?

VII

•   Far as creation's ample range extends,
The scale of sensual, mental powers ascends:
Mark how it mounts, to man's imperial race,
From the green myriads° in the peopled grass: 210
What modes of sight betwixt each wide extreme,
The mole's dim curtain, and the lynx's beam.°
Of smell, the headlong lioness° between,
And hound sagacious° on the tainted° green:
Of hearing, from the life that fills the flood,   215
To that which warbles through the vernal wood:
The spider's touch, how exquisitely fine!
Feels at each thread, and lives along the line:
In the nice bee, what sense so subtly true
From poisonous herbs extract the healing dew?°   220
How instinct varies in the groveling swine,
Compared, half-reasoning elephant, with thine!
'Twixt that, and reason, what a nice barrier;
For ever separate, yet for ever near!
Remembrance and reflection how allied;   225
What thin partitions sense from thought divide:
And middle natures, how they long to join,
Yet never pass th' insuperable line!
Without this just gradation, could they be
Subjected, these to those, or all to thee?   230
The powers of all subdued by thee alone,
Is not thy reason all these powers in one?

VIII

See, through this air, this ocean, and this earth,
All matter quick, and bursting into birth.
Above, how high, progressive life may go!   235
Around, how wide! how deep extend below!
Vast chain of being! which from God began,
Natures ethereal, human, angel, man,

°*myriads:* insects   °*lynx's beam:* the ancient opinion that vision occurs by means
of rays beamed from the eye   °*lioness:* believed to have a dull sense of smell
°*sagacious:* perceptive   °*tainted:* carrying an animal smell   °*healing dew:*
honey

Beast, bird, fish, insect, what no eye can see,
No glass can reach; from Infinite to thee,   240
From thee to nothing.—On superior powers
Were we to press, inferior might on ours:
Or in the full creation leave a void,
Where, one step broken, the great scale's destroyed:
From Nature's chain whatever link you strike,   245
Tenth, or ten thousandth, breaks the chain alike.
　And, if each system in gradation roll
Alike essential to th' amazing whole,
The least confusion but in one, not all
That system only, but the whole must fall.   250
Let earth unbalanced from her orbit fly,
Planets and suns run lawless through the sky;
Let ruling angels from their spheres be hurled,
Being on being wrecked, and world on world;
Heaven's whole foundations to their center nod,   255
And Nature tremble to the throne of God.
All this dread order break—for whom? for thee?
Vile worm!—oh madness! pride! impiety!

IX

What if the foot, ordained the dust to tread,
Or hand, to toil, aspired to be the head?   260
What if the head, the eye, or ear repined
To serve mere engines to the ruling mind?
Just as absurd for any part to claim
To be another, in this general frame:
Just as absurd, to mourn the tasks or pains,   265
The great directing Mind of all ordains.
　All are but parts of one stupendous whole,
Whose body Nature is, and God the soul;
That, changed through all, and yet in all the same;
Great in the earth, as in th' ethereal frame;   270
Warms in the sun, refreshes in the breeze,
Glows in the stars, and blossoms in the trees,
Lives through all life, extends through all extent,
Spreads undivided, operates unspent;
Breathes in our soul, informs our mortal part,   275
As full, as perfect, in a hair as heart;
As full, as perfect, in vile man that mourns,
As the rapt seraph that adores and burns:
To Him no high, no low, no great, no small;
He fills, He bounds, connects, and equals all.   280

Cease then, nor order imperfection name:
Our proper bliss depends on what we blame.
Know thy own point: this kind, this due degree
Of blindness, weakness, Heaven bestows on thee.
Submit.—In this, or any other sphere,   285
Secure to be as blessed as thou canst bear:
Safe in the hand of one disposing Power,
Or in the natal, or the mortal hour.
All Nature is but art, unknown to thee;
All chance, direction, which thou canst not see;   290
All discord, harmony not understood;
All partial evil, universal good:
And, spite of pride, in erring reason's spite,
One truth is clear, Whatever is, is right.

*   *   *

Walt Whitman—American singer, bard, dogmatist, egotist, eccentric, radical, fundamentalist—and his poetry—intense, erotic, sincere—are opposite in almost every way to the decorous elegance of Pope. For Whitman, the Self is God, and creativity, instead of being an expression of God's power, is seen in the energy of the Individual, in that person's particular and unique voice, saying his/her "thing," uttering his/her special cadence and sensibility.

Song of Myself is far from being the subtlest of Romantic poems, but it asserts the basic Romantic point of view firmly and assuredly. It is a poem that expresses the powers of the self without apology or guilt, one in which the self is connected with a huge range of people, things, and kinds of existence outside itself. It is a poem that tries by the intensity and sincerity of its tone to persuade the reader to believe in the strength, quality, and truth of the Self and the Self's opinions that are expressed.

The poem does not bear up under the analytic mode of reading and response, as the sections of the poem reprinted here show. It is the Voice of the Speaker, his Sympathies and Passions, his Fears and Confidences, his Energy and Special Character that should be listened for and thought about.

From SONG OF MYSELF

Walt Whitman (1819–1892)

1

I celebrate myself, and sing myself,
And what I assume you shall assume,
For every atom belonging to me as good belongs to you.

Archetype

I loafe and invite my soul,
I lean and loafe at my ease observing a spear of summer grass.   5

My tongue, every atom of my blood, form'd from this soil, this air,
Born here of parents born here from parents the same, and their parents
    the same,
I, now thirty-seven years old in perfect health begin,
Hoping to cease not till death.

Creeds and schools in abeyance,   10
Retiring back a while sufficed at what they are, but never forgotten,
I harbor for good or bad, I permit to speak at every hazard,
Nature without check with original energy.

2

Houses and rooms are full of perfumes, the shelves are crowded with
    perfumes,   15
I breathe the fragrance myself and know it and like it,
The distillation would intoxicate me also, but I shall not let it.

The atmosphere is not a perfume, it has no taste of the distillation, it is
    odorless,
It is for my mouth forever, I am in love with it,
I will go to the bank by the wood and become undisguised and naked,   20
I am mad for it to be in contact with me.

The smoke of my own breath,
Echoes, ripples, buzz'd whispers, love-root, silk-thread, crotch and vine,
My respiration and inspiration, the beating of my heart, the passing of
    blood and air through my lungs,
The sniff of green leaves and dry leaves, and of the shore and dark-color'd
    sea-rocks, and of hay in the barn,   25

The sound of the belch'd words of my voice loos'd to the eddies of the wind,
A few light kisses, a few embraces, a reaching around of arms,
The play of shine and shade on the trees as the supple boughs wag,
The delight alone or in the rush of the streets, or along the fields and hill-sides.
The feeling of health, the full-noon trill, the song of me rising from bed and meeting the sun. 30

Have you reckon'd a thousand acres much? have you reckon'd the earth much?
Have you practis'd so long to learn to read?
Have you felt so proud to get at the meaning of poems?

Stop this day and night with me and you shall possess the origin of all poems,
You shall possess the good of the earth and sun (there are millions of suns left,) 35
You shall no longer take things at second or third hand, nor look through the eyes of the dead, nor feed on the spectres in books,
You shall not look through my eyes either, nor take things from me,
You shall listen to all sides and filter them from your self.

. . .

13

The negro holds firmly the reins of his four horses, the block swags underneath on its tied-over chain,
The negro that drives the long dray of the stone-yard, steady and tall he stands pois'd on one leg on the string-piece, 40
His blue shirt exposes his ample neck and breast and loosens over his hip-band,
His glance is calm and commanding, he tosses the slouch of his hat away from his forehead,
The sun falls on his crispy hair and mustache, falls on the black of his polish'd and perfect limbs.

I behold the picturesque giant and love him, and I do not stop there,
I go with the team also. 45

In me the caresser of life wherever moving, backward as well as forward sluing,°
To niches aside and junior bending, not a person or object missing,
Absorbing all to myself and for this song.

°*sluing:* turning or moving

Oxen that rattle the yoke and chain or halt in the leafy shade, what is that
   you express in your eyes?
It seems to me more than all the print I have read in my life.   50

My tread scares the wood-drake and wood-duck on my distant and
   day-long ramble,
They rise together, they slowly circle around.

I believe in those wing'd purposes,
And acknowledge red, yellow, white, playing within me,
And consider green and violet and the tufted crown intentional,   55
And do not call the tortoise unworthy because she is not something else,
And the jay in the woods never studied the gamut,° yet trills pretty well to
   me,
And the look of the bay mare shames silliness out of me.

14

The wild gander leads his flock through the cool night,
Ya-honk he says, and sounds it down to me like an invitation,   60
The pert° may suppose it meaningless, but I listening close,
Find its purpose and place up there toward the wintry sky.

The sharp-hoof 'd moose of the north, the cat on the house-sill, the
   chickadee, the prairie-dog,
The litter of the grunting sow as they tug at her teats,
The brood of the turkey-hen and she with her half-spread wings,   65
I see in them and myself the same old law.

The press of my foot to the earth springs a hundred affections,
They scorn the best I can do to relate them.

I am enamour'd of growing out-doors,
Of men that live among cattle or taste of the ocean or woods,   70
Of the builders and steerers of ships and the wielders of axes and mauls,
   and the drivers of horses,
I can eat and sleep with them week in and week out.

What is commonest, cheapest, nearest, easiest, is Me,
Me going in for my chances, spending for vast returns,
Adorning myself to bestow myself on the first that will take me,   75
Not asking the sky to come down to my good will,
Scattering it freely forever.

°*gamut:*   a musical scale   °*pert:*   clever or glib

The pure contralto sings in the organ loft,

The carpenter dresses his plank, the tongue of his foreplane whistles its
wild ascending lisp,

The married and unmarried children ride home to their Thanksgiving
dinner, 80

The pilot seizes the king-pin, he heaves down with a strong arm,

The mate stands braced in the whale-boat, lance and harpoon are ready,

The duck-shooter walks by silent and cautious stretches,

The deacons are ordain'd with cross'd hands at the altar,

The spinning-girl retreats and advances to the hum of the big wheel, 85

The farmer stops by the bars as he walks on a First-day°loafe and looks at
the oats and rye,

The lunatic is carried at last to the asylum a confirm'd case,

(He will never sleep any more as he did in the cot in his mother's
bed-room;)

The jour printer° with gray head and gaunt jaws works at his case,°

He turns his quid of tobacco while his eyes blurr with the manuscript; 90

The malform'd limbs are tied to the surgeon's table,

What is removed drops horribly in a pail;

The quadroon girl is sold at the auction-stand, the drunkard nods by the
bar-room stove,

The machinist rolls up his sleeves, the policeman travels his beat, the
gate-keeper marks who pass,

The young fellow drives the express-wagon (I love him, though I do not
know him;) 95

The half-breed straps on his light boots to compete in the race,

The western turkey-shooting draws old and young, some lean on their
rifles, some sit on logs,

Out from the crowd steps the marksman, takes his position, levels his
piece;

The groups of newly-come immigrants cover the wharf or levee,

As the woolly-pates hoe in the sugar-field, the overseer views them from
his saddle, 100

The bugle calls in the ball-room, the gentlemen run for their partners, the
dancers bow to each other,

The youth lies awake in the cedar-roof'd garret and harks to the musical
rain,

The Wolverine sets traps on the creek that helps fill the Huron,

The squaw wrapt in her yellow-hemm'd cloth is offering moccasins and
bead-bags for sale,

°*First-day:* Quaker usage for Sunday   °*jour printer:* of a daily paper
°*case:* the boxes in which hand-set type is contained

The connoisseur peers along the exhibition-gallery with half-shut eyes
bent sideways,   105
As the deck-hands make fast the steamboat the plank is thrown for the
shore-going passengers,
The young sister holds out the skein while the elder sister winds it off in a
ball, and stops now and then for the knots,
The one-year wife is recovering and happy having a week ago borne her
first child,
The clean-hair'd Yankee girl works with her sewing-machine or in the
factory or mill,
The paving-man leans on his two-handed rammer, the reporter's lead
flies swiftly over the note-book, the sign-painter is lettering with blue
and gold,   110
The canal boy trots on the tow-path, the book-keeper counts at his desk,
the shoemaker waxes his thread,
The conductor beats time for the band and all the performers follow him,
The child is baptized, the convert is making his first professions,
The regatta is spread on the bay, the race is begun (how the white sails
sparkle!)
The drover watching his drove sings out to them that would stray,   115
The pedler sweats with his pack on his back (the purchaser higgling about
the odd cent;)
The bride unrumples her white dress, the minute-hand of the clock
moves slowly,
The opium-eater reclines with rigid head and just-open'd lips,
The prostitute draggles her shawl, her bonnet bobs on her tipsy and
pimpled neck,
The crowd laugh at her blackguard oaths, the men jeer and wink to each
other,   120
(Miserable! I do not laugh at your oaths nor jeer you;)
The President holding a cabinet council is surrounded by the great
Secretaries,
On the piazza walk three matrons stately and friendly with twined arms,
The crew of the fish-smack pack repeated layers of halibut in the hold,
The Missourian crosses the plains toting his wares and his cattle,   125
As the fare-collector goes through the train he gives notice by the jingling
of loose change,
The floor-men are laying the floor, the tinners are tinning the roof, the
masons are calling for mortar,
In single file each shouldering his hod pass onward the laborers;
Seasons pursuing each other the indescribable crowd is gather'd, it is the
fourth of Seventh-month° (what salutes of cannon and small arms!)

°*Seventh-month:* July

Seasons pursuing each other the plougher ploughs, the mower mows, and
 the winter-grain falls in the ground;   130
Off on the lakes the pike-fisher watches and waits by the hole in the frozen
 surface,
The stumps stand thick round the clearing, the squatter strikes deep with
 his axe,
Flatboatmen make fast towards dusk near the cotton-wood or
 pecan-trees,
Coon-seekers go through the regions of the Red river or through those
 drain'd by the Tennessee, or through those of the Arkansas,
Torches shine in the dark that hangs on the Chattahooche or
 Altamahaw,   135
Patriarchs sit at supper with sons and grandsons and great-grandsons
 around them,
In walls of adobie, in canvas tents, rest hunters and trappers after their
 day's sport,
The city sleeps and the country sleeps,
The living sleep for their time, the dead sleep for their time,
The old husband sleeps by his wife and the young husband sleeps by his
 wife;   140
And these tend inward to me, and I tend outward to them,
And such as it is to be of these more or less I am,
And of these one and all I weave the song of myself.

16

I am of old and young, of the foolish as much as the wise,
Regardless of others, ever regardful of others,   145
Maternal as well as paternal, a child as well as a man,
Stuff 'd with the stuff that is coarse and stuff'd with the stuff that is fine,
One of the Nation of many nations, the smallest the same and the largest
 the same,
A Southerner soon as a Northerner, a planter nonchalant and hospitable
 down by the Oconee I live,
A Yankee bound my own way ready for trade, my joints the limberest
 joints on earth and the sternest joints on earth,   150
A Kentuckian walking the vale of the Elkhorn in my deerskin leggings, a
 Louisianian or Georgian,
A boatman over lakes or bays or along coasts, a Hoosier, Badger, Buckeye;
At home on Kanadian snow-shoes or up in the bush, or with fishermen off
 Newfoundland,
At home in the fleet of ice-boats, sailing with the rest and tacking,
At home on the hills of Vermont or in the woods of Maine, or the Texan
 ranch,   155

Comrade of Californians, comrade of free North-Westerners (loving
    their big proportions,)
Comrade of raftsmen and coalmen, comrade of all who shake hands and
    welcome to drink and meat,
A learner with the simplest, a teacher of the thoughtfullest,
A novice beginning yet experient of myriads of seasons,
Of every hue and caste am I, of every rank and religion,   160
A farmer, mechanic, artist, gentleman, sailor, quaker,
Prisoner, fancy-man, rowdy, lawyer, physician, priest.

I resist any thing better than my own diversity,
Breathe the air but leave plenty after me,
And am not stuck up, and am in my place.   165

(The moth and the fish-eggs are in their place,
The bright suns I see and the dark suns I cannot see are in their place,
The palpable is in its place and the impalpable is in its place.)

17

These are really the thoughts of all men in all ages and lands, they are not
    original with me,
If they are not yours as much as mine they are nothing, or next to
    nothing,   170
If they are not the riddle and the untying of the riddle they are nothing,
If they are not just as close as they are distant they are nothing.

This is the grass that grows wherever the land is and the water is,
This is the common air that bathes the globe.

18

With music strong I come, with my cornets and my drums,   175
I play not marches for accepted victors only, I play marches for conquer'd
    and slain persons.

Have you heard that it was good to gain the day?
I also say it is good to fall, battles are lost in the same spirit in which they
    are won.

I beat and pound for the dead,
I blow through my embouchures° my loudest and gayest for them.   180

°*embouchures:*   mouthpieces, presumably for bugles or trumpets

Vivas to those who have fail'd!
And to those whose war-vessels sank in the sea!
And to those themselves who sank in the sea!
And to all generals that lost engagements, and all overcome heroes!
And the numberless unknown heroes equal to the greatest heroes known! 185

19

This is the meal equally set, this the meat for natural hunger,
It is for the wicked just the same as the righteous, I make appointments
  with all.
I will not have a single person slighted or left away,
The kept-woman, sponger, thief, are hereby invited,
The heavy-lipp'd slave is invited, the venerealee° is invited;   190
There shall be no difference between them and the rest.

This is the press of a bashful hand, this the float and odor of hair,
This the touch of my lips to yours, this the murmur of yearning,
This the far-off depth and height reflecting my own face,
This the thoughtful merge of myself, and the outlet again.   195

Do you guess I have some intricate purpose?
Well I have, for the Fourth-month showers have, and the mica on the side
  of a rock has.

Do you take it I would astonish?
Does the daylight astonish? does the early redstart twittering through the
  woods?
Do I astonish more than they?   200

This hour I tell things in confidence,
I might not tell everybody, but I will tell you.

Who goes there? hankering, gross, mystical, nude;
How is it I extract strength from the beef I eat?

What is a man anyhow? what am I? what are you?   205

All I mark as my own you shall offset it with your own,
Else it were time lost listening to me.

I do not snivel that snivel the world over,
That months are vacuums and the ground but wallow and filth.

°*venerealee:*   a person interested in sexual activity

Whimpering and truckling fold with powders for invalids, conformity
goes to the fourth-remov'd,   210
I wear my hat as I please indoors or out.

Why should I pray? why should I venerate and be ceremonious?

Having pried through the strata, analyzed to a hair, counsel'd with
doctors and calculated close,
I find no sweeter fat than sticks to my own bones.

In all people I see myself, none more and not one a barleycorn less,   215
And the good or bad I say of myself I say of them.

I know I am solid and sound,
To me the converging objects of the universe perpetually flow,
All are written to me, and I must get what the writing means.

I know I am deathless,   220
I know this orbit of mine cannot be swept by a carpenter's compass,
I know I shall not pass like a child's carlacue cut with a burnt stick at night.

I know I am august,
I do not trouble my spirit to vindicate itself or be understood,
I see that the elementary laws never apologize,   225
(I reckon I behave no prouder than the level I plant my house by, after
all.)

I exist as I am, that is enough,
If no other in the world be aware I sit content,
And if each and all be aware I sit content.

One world is aware and by far the largest to me, and that is myself,   230
And whether I come to my own to-day or in ten thousand or ten million
years,
I can cheerfully take it now, or with equal cheerfulness I can wait.

My foothold is tenon'd and mortis'd° in granite,
I laugh at what you call dissolution,
And I know the amplitude of time.   235

. . .

°*tenon'd and mortis'd:*   firmly set, as in a carpenter's joint

I am the teacher of athletes,
He that by me spreads a wider breast than my own proves the width of my
    own,
He most honors my style who learns under it to destroy the teacher.

The boy I love, the same becomes a man not through derived power but in
    his own right,
Wicked rather than virtuous out of conformity or fear.   240
Fond of his sweetheart, relishing well his steak,
Unrequited love or a slight cutting him worse than sharp steel cuts,
First-rate to ride, to fight, to hit the bull's eye, to sail a skiff, to sing a song
    or play on the banjo,
Preferring scars and the beard and faces pitted with small-pox over all
    latherers,°
And those well-tann'd to those that keep out of the cold.   245

I teach straying from me, yet who can stray from me?
I follow you whoever you are from the present hour,
My words itch at your ears till you understand them.

I do not say these things for a dollar or to fill up the time while I wait for a
    boat,
(It is you talking just as much as myself, I act as the tongue of you,   250
Tied in your mouth, in mine it begins to be loosen'd.)

I swear I will never again mention love or death inside the house,
And I swear I will never translate° myself at all, only to him or her who
    privately stays with me in the open air.

If you would understand me go to the heights or watery shore,
The nearest gnat is an explanation, and a drop or motion of waves a key, 255
The maul, the oar, the hand-saw, second my words.

No shutter'd room or school can commune with me,
But roughs and little children better than they.

The young mechanic is closest to me, he knows me well,
The woodman that takes his axe and jug with him shall take me with him
    all day,   260
The farm-boy ploughing in the field feels good at the sound of my
    voice,

°*latherers:*   people who are clean shaven   °*translate:*   explain

In vessels that sail my words sail, I go with fishermen and seamen and love them.

The soldier camp'd or upon the march is mine,
On the night ere the pending battle many seek me, and I do not fail them,
On that solemn night (it might be their last) those that know me seek me. 265

My face rubs to the hunter's face when he lies down alone in his blanket,
The driver thinking of me does not mind the jolt of his wagon,
The young mother and old mother comprehend me,
The girl and the wife rest the needle a moment and forget where they are,
They and all would resume° what I have told them. 270

I have said that the soul is not more than the body,
And I have said that the body is not more than the soul,
And nothing, not God, is greater to one than one's self is,
And whoever walks a furlong without sympathy walks to his own funeral drest in his shroud,
And I or you pocketless of a dime may purchase the pick of the earth, 275
And to glance with an eye or show a bean in its pod confounds the learning of all times,
And there is no trade or employment but the young man following it may become a hero,
And there is no object so soft but it makes a hub for the wheel'd universe,
And I say to any man or woman, Let your soul stand cool and composed before a million universes.

And I say to mankind, Be not curious about God, 280
For I who am curious about each am not curious about God,
(No array of terms can say how much I am at peace about God and about death.)

I hear and behold God in every object, yet understand God not in the least,
Nor do I understand who there can be more wonderful than myself.

Why should I wish to see God better than this day? 285
I see something of God each hour of the twenty-four, and each moment then,
In the faces of men and women I see God, and in my own face in the glass,
I find letters from God dropt in the street, and every one is sign'd by God's name,
And I leave them where they are, for I know that wheresoe'er I go,
Others will punctually come for ever and ever. 290

°*resume:* summarize or remember

And as to you Death, and you bitter hug of mortality, it is idle to try to alarm me.

To his work without flinching the accoucheur° comes,
I see the elder-hand° pressing receiving supporting,
I recline by the sills of the exquisite flexible doors,
And mark the outlet, and mark the relief and escape.   295

And as to you Corpse I think you are good manure, but that does not offend me,
I smell the white roses sweet-scented and growing,
I reach to the leafy lips, I reach to the polish'd breasts of melons.

And as to you Life I reckon you are the leavings of many deaths,
(No doubt I have died myself ten thousand times before.)   300

I hear you whispering there O stars of heaven,
O suns—O grass of graves—O perpetual transfers and promotions,
If you do not say any thing how can I say any thing?

Of the turbid pool that lies in the autumn forest,
Of the moon that descends the steeps of the soughing twilight,   305
Toss, sparkles of day and dusk—toss on the black stems that decay in the muck,
Toss to the moaning gibberish of the dry limbs.

I ascend from the moon, I ascend from the night,
I perceive that the ghastly glimmer is noonday sunbeams reflected,
And debouch° to the steady and central from the offspring great or small. 310

50

There is that in me—I do not know what it is—but I know it is in me.

Wrench'd and sweaty—calm and cool then my body becomes,
I sleep—I sleep long.

I do not know it—it is without name—it is a word unsaid,
It is not in any dictionary, utterance, symbol.   315

°*accoucheur:* obstetrician   °*elder-hand:* uncertain: perhaps a midwife or attendant   °*debouch:* march out

Something it swings on more than the earth I swing on,
To it the creation is the friend whose embracing awakes me.

Perhaps I might tell more. Outlines! I plead for my brothers and sisters.

Do you see O my brothers and sisters?
It is not chaos or death — it is form, union, plan — it is eternal life — it is
    Happiness.   320

51

The past and present wilt — I have fill'd them, emptied them,
And proceed to fill my next fold of the future.

Listener up there! what have you to confide to me?
Look in my face while I snuff the sidle° of evening,
(Talk honestly, no one else hears you, and I stay only a minute longer.) 325

Do I contradict myself?
Very well then I contradict myself,
(I am large, I contain multitudes.)

I concentrate toward them that are nigh, I wait on the door-slab.

Who has done his day's work? who will soonest be through with his
    supper?   330
Who wishes to walk with me?

Will you speak before I am gone? will you prove already too late?

52

The spotted hawk swoops by and accuses me, he complains of my gab and
    my loitering.

I too am not a bit tamed, I too am untranslatable,
I sound my barbaric yawp over the roofs of the world.   335

The last scud of day holds back for me,
It flings my likeness after the rest and true as any on the shadow'd wilds,
It coaxes me to the vapor and the dusk.

°*sidle:* a sidewise movement, as an evening breeze

I depart as air, I shake my white locks at the runaway sun,
I effuse my flesh in eddies, and drift it in lacy jags.   340

I bequeath myself to the dirt to grow from the grass I love,
If you want me again look for me under your boot-soles.

You will hardly know who I am or what I mean,
But I shall be good health to you nevertheless,
And filter and fibre your blood.   345

Falling to fetch me at first keep encouraged,
Missing me one place search another,
I stop somewhere waiting for you.

                                *   *   *

John Stuart Mill, one of the leading philosophers of the 19th century, perceived very early and very accurately the leading "tendencies of thought," as he called them, involved in the Romantic Movement, the points of distinction that it contained, and the points at which it rejected views of the previous century. His own lengthy comments on the distinction can be found by reading and comparing two essays, one on Jeremy Bentham, whom he took to be the best representative of the old point of view, the other on Samuel Taylor Coleridge, whom Mill saw as the leading exponent of the modern state of mind.

A shorter summary of the differences is contained in the following account of the ways in which these fundamental questions are reflected in the poets of a particular age. When Mill speaks of a Royalist or a Conservative poet, he speaks of what we have been calling Traditional or Classical; when he speaks of the Radical or Movement poet, he refers to what we have been calling Romantic.

From POEMS AND ROMANCES OF ALFRED de VIGNY, 1838

John Stuart Mill (1806–1873)

CONSERVATIVE AND MOVEMENT POETS

It may be worth while to employ a moment in considering what are the general features which, in an age of revolutions, may be expected to distinguish a Royalist or Conservative from a Liberal or Radical poet or imaginative writer. . . . The pervading spirit, then, of the one, will be love of the Past; of the other, faith in the Future. The partialities of the one will be towards things established, settled, regulated; of the other, towards human free will, cramped and fettered in all directions, both for good and ill, by those establishments and regulations. Both will have a heroic sympathy with heroism, for both are poets; but the one will respond most readily to the heroism of endurance and self-control, the other to that of strength and struggle. Of the virtues and beauties of our common humanity, the one will view with most affection those which have their natural growth under the shelter of fixed habits and firmly settled opinions: local and family attachments, tranquil tastes and pleasures, those gentle and placid feelings towards man and nature, ever most easy to those upon whom is not imposed the burthen of being their own protectors and their own guides. A greater spirit of reverence, deeper humility, the virtues of abnegation and forbearance carried to a higher degree, will distinguish his favorite personages: while, as subjection to a common faith and law brings the most diverse characters to the same standard, and tends more or less to efface their differences, a certain monotony of goodness will be apparent, and a degree of distaste for *prononcé*° characters, as being near allied to ill-regulated ones. The sympathies of the Radical or Movement poet will take the opposite direction. Active qualities are what he will demand rather than passive; those which fit men for making changes in circumstances which surround them, rather than for accommodating themselves to those circumstances. Sensible he must of course be of the necessity of restraints but being dissatisfied with those which exist, his dislike of established opinions and institutions turns naturally into sympathy with all things, not in themselves bad, which those opinions and institutions restrain, that is, for all natural human feelings. Free and vigorous developments of human nature, even when he cannot refuse them his disapprobation, will command his sympathy: a more marked individuality will usually be conspicuous in his creations; his heroic characters will be all armed for conflict, full of energy and strong self-will, of grand conceptions and brilliant virtues, but in habits of virtue, often below those of the Conservative school: there will not be so broad and black a line between his good and bad personages; his characters of principle will be more tolerant of his characters of mere passion. Among human affections, the Conservative poet will give the preference to those which can be invested with the character of duties; to those of which the objects are as it were marked but by the arrangements of nature, we ourselves exercising no choice: as the parental—the filial—the conjugal *after* the irrevocable union, or a solemn betrothment equivalent to it, and with due observance of all decencies, both real and conventional. The other will delight in painting the affections which choose their own objects, especially the most powerful of these, passionate love; and of that, the more vehement

°*prononcé:* strongly individualized

oftener than the more graceful aspects; will select by preference its subtlest workings, and its most unusual and unconventional forms; will show
it at war with the forms and customs of society, nay even with its laws and
its religion, if the laws and tenets which regulate that branch of human
relations are among those which have begun to be murmured against. By
the Conservative, feelings and states of mind which he disapproves will be
indicated rather than painted; to lay open the morbid anatomy of human
nature will appear to him contrary to good taste always, and often to
morality: and inasmuch as feelings intense enough to threaten established
decorums with any danger of violation will most frequently have the
character of morbidness in his eyes, the representation of passion in the
colours of reality will commonly be left to the Movement poet. To him,
whatever exists will appear, from that alone, fit to be represented: to
probe the wounds of society and humanity is part of his business, and he
will neither shrink from exhibiting what is in nature, because it is morally
culpable, nor because it is physically revolting. Even in their representations of inanimate nature there will be a difference. The picture
most grateful and most familiar to the one will be those of a universe at
peace within itself—of stability and duration—of irresistible power
serenely at rest, or moving in fulfilment of the established arrangements
of the universe: whatever suggests unity of design, and the harmonious
co-operation of all the forces of nature towards the end intended by a
Being in whom there is no variableness nor shadow of change. In the
creations of the other, nature will oftener appear in the relations which it
bears to the individual rather than to the scheme of the universe; there
will be a larger place assigned to those of its aspects which reflect back the
troubles of an unquiet soul, the impulses of a passionate, or the
enjoyments of a voluptuous one; and on the whole, here too the Movement poet will extend so much more widely the bounds of the permitted,
that his sources, both of effect and of permanent interest, will have a far
larger range; and he will generally be more admired than the other, by all
those by whom he is not actually condemned.

There is room in the world for poets of both these kinds; and the
greatest will always partake of the nature of both. A comprehensive and
catholic mind and heart will doubtless feel and exhibit all these different
sympathies, each in its due proportion and degree; but what the due
proportion may happen to be, is part of the larger question which every
one has to ask of himself at such periods, viz. whether it were for the good
of humanity at the particular era, that Conservative or Radical feeling
should most predominate? For there is a perpetual antagonism between
these two; and, until all things are as well ordered as they can ever be, each
will require to be in a greater or less degree, tempered by the other: nor
until the ordinances of law and of opinion are so framed as to give full
scope to all individuality not positively noxious, and to restrain all that is
noxious, will the two classes of sympathies ever be entirely reconciled.

QUESTIONS

1. Pope offers a variety of arguments and illustrations of his point of view. Which ones seem most convincing? Which least? Why?

2. Pride, the first of the deadly sins, Satan's sin in rebelling against God, is seen by Pope as the chief cause of human unhappiness. Explain the reasons Pope gives for taking this view. Why do we often think it acceptable to take pride in something?

3. The traditional view emphasizes proper attitudes toward authority. What authorities does Pope see as most important, and what harm does he suppose comes from failure to observe them? Suggest a rebuttal to this argument that would assert the rights of the individual.

4. Nature in the Classical view is usually orderly, full of design, and coherence. What use does Pope make of Nature in his argument? What kind of examples does he like? What other views of Nature are there, and what other evidence does Nature present that is not given in this poem?

5. This poem makes a great show of logical method. Analyze the logical constructions and show their strength or weakness.

6. The most difficult question for someone arguing this position is to explain the existence of injustice, evil, and error in the world. How does Pope deal with these questions?

7. The last 28 lines (267ff.) are often described as a good summary account of Classicism and tradition and should be kept in mind as a point of reference. What degree of conviction or dissent do you have about it?

8. Nature plays an important role in *Song of Myself*. What kinds of natural situations and images does Whitman use most often? What position does he like in relation to the natural world?

9. In Section 2 Whitman talks about the Romantic view of poetry, saying that if the reader "stops" with him, he will "possess the origin of all poems." What quality of poetic discourse does he emphasize in this passage, and what kind of poetry should it produce?

10. Sections 15 and 16 are organized on the principle of the grocery list. What does Whitman try to emphasize by listing these occupations and human conditions? Notice the contrasts and juxtapositions. What is the thing about each one that he picks out for emphasis? If Romantic art emphasizes the Self as apart from external values, how can a Romantic be such a democrat?

11. Section 19 emphasizes Whitman's distaste for apology, for whimpering and truckling, and for prayer. Why do these states of mind appear so distasteful to him?

12. The last five sections (48–52) refer most specifically to religion. What is Whitman's idea of God? What does the Romantic feel about God? Can a Romantic such as Whitman be called religious? Why or why not?

13. Section 48 emphasizes the idea of sympathy among people. Why is this idea important to Whitman? What ideas earlier in the poem have led to this statement?

14. Sincerity is the key to Whitman's effort to move the reader. What are some of the techniques Whitman uses to indicate the authenticity of his statements? Readers tend to be clear on whether they like and believe this voice or whether they mistrust and disbelieve its sincerity. Why does there seem to be small ground for compromise between these two views?

15. Whitman's openness gives plain opportunity to see the moral and intellectual weaknesses or dangers of the Romantic position. What are some of the objections and questions that this view might raise?

16. List the fundamental distinctions made by Mill between the Conservative (Classical) poet and the Radical (Romantic) poet in regard to politics, society, the past, people's characters, families, feelings, Nature.

17. Notice that Mill sees a "perpetual antagonism" between these two kinds of poets. What is the basis of the assumption? What view of society and history is involved?

PART III

The Romantic Consciousness

The Romantic Consciousness

Thus far we have seen that Romanticism represents a distinct change in the intellectual history of Western Europe, and we have gained some sense of the particular values it represents. It is not surprising to discover that these changes and the new kinds of literary expression they produced did not occur without struggle and pain. The account of this process in the minds of poets and philosophers forms an important part of Romantic literature.

The Dark Night of the Soul

The pattern of this story is simple and familiar, one that will be recognized as applying not only to Romantic Selves facing a new Reality but also in a less dramatic way to most thoughtful people whose coming of age, whose recognition of the historical and psychological forces that affect their lives, is accompanied by turmoil and struggle.

The story takes its basic form from the Faust myth: A person with superior powers, overconfident and full of pride in his intellectual achievements and ready to use the power of science and analytic reason to destroy error and superstition and tradition, discovers that in the course of ridding himself of his past, his dependence on his parents and on convention, he has acquired a monster, has created a sorcerer's apprentice, whose powers may be illimitable. Potent against old beliefs, it will not stop when bidden but continue to devour not only old beliefs but *all* beliefs. Throwing off the errors of the past leaves one with new problems and creates a state of psychological despair, a Dark Night of the Soul in which the Self and its very existence, its Freedom to Choose and Be, loses validity. The person then suffers pains and anxieties that the old restraints had prevented. By defining what was right and wrong, the social and moral conventions of the old tradition imposed constraints on individual behavior in the name of Order and Design. If these values are rejected, something must be found to take their place. The Romantic Self suffers a terrible loss when it discovers that the means by which the hold on the old values was loosened can affect the strength of the new values as well.

The old superstition and tradition were thrown off by means of rational analysis. Religion and the power of royal authority lose their sanctity, their special condition. The king is a political man; his neck may be placed in a guillotine. However, rational habits of mind, although they produce these revolutionary freedoms, continue to produce skepticism and doubt, and to offer negative criticism of values. The new values of freedom, individuality, and Democracy are as liable to these destructive processes as were the old ideas of Constraint, Order, Social Stability, and God's Providence. One cannot look analytically at the psychological origins of faith and love or at the motives for programs of social improvement and remain a faithful, loving friend or a devoted philosopher or politician. The Enlightenment discovered Reason, and Reason, having dispelled the old mystery, continued searching for the new causes of things, leading the Self into a nightmarish existence, into a world filled entirely with rationality, where all behavior is the result of mechanical sequences of cause and effect, where all belief, emotion, and assertion are without ultimate causes, where all can be analyzed and explained "away" according to some social, biological, psychological, or chemical theory.

This condition is serious and deadly; it is what we would now call, not very precisely, a nervous breakdown, or depression. In this condition there is hostility toward the Self, absence of confidence, and loss of will. Other people who had been objects of lively animated feelings and sources of emotion are seen as being mechanical, blind automata, functioning without spirit in a universe of dead, mechanical causes and effects. Goals and aspirations are seen as being arbitrary and useless, one as good or as bad as another. Moral judgments are all relative. People become mechanisms to be "turned on." "Whatever turns you on" is as good as anything else. Money, Power, Goodness, Success, Sexual Connections are all subject to analysis and become equally arbitrary and worthless. The alienation, despair, and desperation that this condition produces is a common and admonitory theme in Romantic art. If we are led to admire Romantic values, we should pay careful attention to the danger.

*   *   *

John Stuart Mill's *Autobiography* recounts the intellectual events of his development from a precocious youth to being the leading voice of rationalism and liberal politics of the 19th century. Part of that account is his description of his dark night of the soul, which provides a striking example of the change in consciousness from traditional Enlightenment psychology to a Romantic sense of self.

Mill was brought up according to strict associationist psychology, in which one learned to associate the idea of one's own happiness with the idea of the happiness of others. Those ideas and feelings were judged best that had the most utility in achieving these social goals. The term *Utilitarianism* was given to moral theories based on this idea. However, at age 20, Mill became unable to believe in the connection between his own happiness and that of others. Suffering this problem, he ceased for a period to be able to feel any interest in others, and he felt himself to be alienated, lonely, and without any meaningful reason for continuing his life.

From AUTOBIOGRAPHY

John Stuart Mill (1806–1873)

From the winter of 1821, when I first read Bentham,° and especially from the commencement of the *Westminster Review,*° I had what might truly be called an object in life: to be a reformer of the world. My conception of my own happiness was entirely identified with this object. The personal sympathies I wished for were those of fellow labourers in this enterprise. I endeavoured to pick up as many flowers as I could by the way; but as a serious and permanent personal satisfaction to rest upon, my whole reliance was placed on this; and I was accustomed to felicitate myself on the certainty of a happy life which I enjoyed, through placing my happiness in something durable and distant, in which some progress might be always making, while it could never be exhausted by complete attainment. This did very well for several years, during which the general improvement going on in the world and the idea of myself as engaged with others in struggling to promote it, seemed enough to fill up an interesting and animated existence. But the time came when I awakened from this as from a dream. It was in the autumn of 1826. I was in a dull state of nerves, such as everybody is occasionally liable to; unsusceptible to enjoyment or pleasurable excitement; one of those moods when what is pleasure at other times, becomes insipid or indifferent; the state, I should think, in which converts to Methodism usually are, when smitten by their first "conviction of sin." In this frame of mind it occurred to me to put the question directly to myself: "Suppose that all your objects in life were realized; that all the changes in institutions and opinions which you are looking forward to, could be completely effected at this very instant: would this be a great joy and happiness to you?" And an irrepressible self-consciousness distinctly answered, "No!" At this my heart sank within me: the whole foundation on which my life was constructed fell down. All my happiness was to have been found in the continual pursuit of this end. The end had ceased to charm, and how could there ever again be any interest in the means? I seemed to have nothing left to live for.

At first I hoped that the cloud would pass away of itself; but it did not. A night's sleep, the sovereign remedy for the smaller vexations of life, had no effect on it. I awoke to a renewed consciousness of the woeful fact. I

°*Bentham:* Jeremy Bentham, 1748–1832, economist, philosopher, founder of Utilitarianism, and friend of Mill's father   °*Westminster Review:* a journal for liberal political theory, to which Mill contributed

carried it with me into all companies, into all occupations. Hardly anything had power to cause me even a few minutes' oblivion of it. For some months the cloud seemed to grow thicker and thicker. The lines in Coleridge's "Dejection"—I was not then acquainted with them—exactly describe my case:

> A grief without a pang, void, dark and drear,
> A drowsy, stifled, unimpassioned grief,
> Which finds no natural outlet or relief
> In word, or sigh, or tear.°

In vain I sought relief from my favourite books; those memorials of past nobleness and greatness from which I had always hitherto drawn strength and animation. I read them now without feeling, or with the accustomed feeling *minus* all its charm; and I became persuaded that my love of mankind, and of excellence for its own sake, had worn itself out. I sought no comfort by speaking to others of what I felt. If I had loved any one sufficiently to make confiding my griefs a necessity, I should not have been in the condition I was. I felt, too, that mine was not an interesting, or in any way respectable distress. There was nothing in it to attract sympathy. Advice, if I had known where to seek it, would have been most precious. The words of Macbeth to the physician often occurred to my thoughts.° But there was no one on whom I could build the faintest hope of such assistance. My father, to whom it would have been natural to me to have recourse in any practical difficulties, was the last person to whom, in such a case as this, I looked for help. Everything convinced me that he had no knowledge of any such mental state as I was suffering from, and that even if he could be made to understand it, he was not the physician who could heal it. My education, which was wholly his work, had been conducted without any regard to the possibility of its ending in this result; and I saw no use in giving him the pain of thinking that his plans had failed, when the failure was probably irremediable, and, at all events, beyond the power of *his* remedies. Of other friends, I had at that time none to whom I had any hope of making my condition intelligible. It was however abundantly intelligible to myself; and the more I dwelt upon it, the more hopeless it appeared.

My course of study had led me to believe that all mental and moral feelings and qualities, whether of a good or of a bad kind, were the results

---

°See Part IV for the full text of this poem.
°*Macbeth* (V, iii, 40-44):
    Canst thou not minister to a mind diseased,
    Pluck from the memory a rooted sorrow,
    Raze out the written troubles of the brain,
    And with some sweet oblivious antidote
    Cleanse the stuffed bosom of that perilous stuff
    Which weighs upon the heart?

of association; that we love one thing, and hate another, take pleasure in one sort of action or contemplation, and pain in another sort, through the clinging of pleasurable or painful ideas to those things, from the effect of education or of experience. As a corollary from this, I had always heard it maintained by my father, and was myself convinced, that the object of education should be to form the strongest possible associations of the salutary class; associations of pleasure with all things beneficial to the great whole, and of pain with all things hurtful to it. This doctrine appeared inexpugnable; but it now seemed to me, on retrospect, that my teachers had occupied themselves but superficially with the means of forming and keeping up these salutary associations. They seemed to have trusted altogether to the old familiar instruments, praise and blame, reward and punishment. Now, I did not doubt that by these means, begun early, and applied unremittingly, intense associations of pain and pleasure, especially of pain, might be created, and might produce desires and aversions capable of lasting undiminished to the end of life. But there must always be something artificial and casual in associations thus produced. The pains and pleasures thus forcibly associated with things, are not connected with them by any natural tie, and it is therefore, I thought, essential to the durability of these associations that they should have become so intense and inveterate as to be practically indissoluble, before the habitual exercise of the power of analysis had commenced. For I now saw, or thought I saw, what I had always before received with incredulity—that the habit of analysis has a tendency to wear away the feelings: as indeed, it has, when no other mental habit is cultivated, and the analysing spirit remains without its natural complements and correctives. The very excellence of analysis (I argued) is that it tends to weaken and undermine whatever is the result of prejudice; that it enables us mentally to separate ideas which have only casually clung together: and no associations whatever could ultimately resist this dissolving force, were it not that we owe to analysis our clearest knowledge of the permanent sequences in nature; the real connexions between Things, not dependent on our will and feelings; natural laws, by virtue of which, in many cases, one thing is inseparable from another in fact; which laws, in proportion as they are clearly perceived and imaginatively realized, cause our ideas of things which are always joined together in Nature, to cohere more and more closely in our thoughts. Analytic habits may thus even strengthen the associations between causes and effects, means and ends, but tend altogether to weaken those which are, to speak familiarly, a *mere* matter of feelings. They are therefore (I thought) favourable to prudence and clear-sightedness, but a perpetual worm at the root both of the passions and of the virtues; and, above all, fearfully undermine all desires, and all pleasures, which are the effects of association, that is, according to the theory I held, all except the purely physical and organic; of the entire insufficiency of which to make life desirable, no one had a stronger conviction than I had. These were the laws of human nature, by which, as it seemed to me, I had been brought to my present state. All those to whom I looked up were of opinion that the pleasure of sympathy with human beings, and the feelings which made the good of others, and especially of mankind on a large scale, the object of existence, were the greatest and surest sources of happiness. Of the truth of this I was convinced, but to know that a feeling would make me happy if I had it, did not give me the feeling. My education, I thought, had failed to create these feelings in sufficient strength to resist the dissolving influence of analysis, while the whole course of my intellectual cultivation had made precocious and premature analysis the inveterate habit of my mind. I was thus, as I said to myself, stranded at the commencement of my voyage, with a well-equipped ship and a rudder, but no sail; without any real desire for the ends which I had been so carefully fitted out to work for: no delight in virtue, or the general good, but also just as little in anything else. The fountains of vanity and ambition seemed to have dried up within me, as completely as those of benevolence. I had had (as I reflected) some gratification of vanity at too early an age: I had obtained some distinction, and felt myself of some importance, before the desire of distinction and of importance had grown into a passion: and little as it was which I had attained, yet having been attained too early, like all pleasures enjoyed too soon, it had made me *blasé* and indifferent to the pursuit. Thus neither selfish nor unselfish pleasures were pleasures to me. And there seemed no power in nature sufficient to begin the formation of my character anew, and create in a mind now irretrievably analytic, fresh associations of pleasure with any of the objects of human desire.

These were the thoughts which mingled with the dry heavy dejection of the melancholy winter of 1826-7. During this time I was not incapable of my usual occupations. I went on with them mechanically, by the mere force of habit. I had been so drilled in a certain sort of mental exercise, that I could still carry it on when all the spirit had gone out of it. I even composed and spoke several speeches at the debating society, how, or with what degree of success, I know not. Of four years continual speaking at that society, this is the only year of which I remember next to nothing. Two lines of Coleridge, in whom alone of all writers I have found a true description of what I felt, were often in my thoughts, not at this time (for I had never read them), but in a later period of the same mental malady:

> Work without hope draws nectar in a sieve,
> And hope without an object cannot live.

In all probability my case was by no means so peculiar as I fancied it, and I doubt not that many others have passed through a similar state; but the idiosyncrasies of my education had given to the general phenomenon a special character, which made it seem the natural effect of causes that it was hardly possible for time to remove. I frequently asked myself, if I could, or if I was bound to go on living, when life must be passed in this manner. I generally answered to myself, that I did not think I could possibly bear it beyond a year. When, however, not more than half that duration of time had elapsed, a small ray of light broke in upon my gloom. I was reading, accidentally, Marmontel's "Memoires," and came to the passage which relates his father's death, the distressed position of the family, and the sudden inspiration by which he, then a mere boy, felt and made them feel that he would be everything to them—would supply the place of all that they had lost. A vivid conception of the scene and its feelings came over me, and I was moved to tears. From this moment my burden grew lighter. The oppression of the thought that all feeling was dead within me, was gone. I was no longer hopeless: I was not a stock or a stone. I had still, it seemed, some of the material out of which all worth of character, and all capacity for happiness, are made. Relieved from my ever present sense of irremediable wretchedness, I gradually found that the ordinary incidents of life could again give me some pleasure; that I could again find enjoyment, not intense, but sufficient for cheerfulness, in sunshine and sky, in books, in conversation, in public affairs; and that there was, once more, excitement, though of a moderate kind, in exerting myself for my opinions, and for the public good. Thus the cloud gradually drew off, and I again enjoyed life: and though I had several relapses, some of which lasted many months, I never again was as miserable as I had been.

The experiences of this period had two very marked effects on my opinions and character. In the first place, they led me to adopt a theory of life very unlike that on which I had before acted, and having much in common with what at that time I certainly had never heard of, the anti-self-consciousness theory of Carlyle. I never, indeed, wavered in the conviction that happiness is the test of all rules of conduct, and the end of life. But I now thought that this end was only to be attained by not making it the direct end. Those only are happy (I thought) who have their minds fixed on some object other than their own happiness; on the happiness of others, on the improvement of mankind, even on some art or pursuit, followed not as a means, but as itself an ideal end. Aiming thus at something else, they find happiness by the way. The enjoyments of life (such was now my theory) are sufficient to make it a pleasant thing, when they are taken *en passant*, without being made a principal object. Once make them so, and they are immediately felt to be insufficient. They will not bear a scrutinizing examination. Ask yourself whether you are happy, and you cease to be so. The only chance is to treat, not happiness, but some end external to it, as the purpose of life. Let your self-consciousness, your scrutiny, your self-interrogation, exhaust themselves on that; and if otherwise fortunately circumstanced you will inhale happiness with the air you breathe, without dwelling on it or thinking about it, without either forestalling it in imagination, or putting it to flight by fatal questioning. This theory now became the basis of my philosophy of life. And I still hold to it as the best theory for all those who have but a moderate degree of sensibility and of capacity for enjoyment, that is, for the great majority of mankind.

The other important change which my opinions at this time underwent, was that I, for the first time, gave its proper place, among the prime necessities of human well-being, to the internal culture of the individual. I ceased to attach almost exclusive importance to the ordering of outward circumstances, and the training of the human being for speculation and for action. I had now learnt by experience that the passive susceptibilities needed to be cultivated as well as the active capacities, and required to be nourished and enriched as well as guided. I did not, for an instant, lose sight of, or undervalue, that part of the truth which I had seen before; I never turned recreant to intellectual culture, or ceased to consider the power and practice of analysis as an essential condition both of individual and of social improvement. But I thought that it had consequences which required to be corrected, by joining other kinds of cultivation with it. The maintenance of a due balance among the faculties now seemed to me of primary importance. The cultivation of the feelings became one of the cardinal points in my ethical and philosophical creed. And my thoughts and inclinations turned in an increasing degree towards whatever seemed capable of being instrumental to that object.

I now began to find meaning in the things which I had read or heard about the importance of poetry and art as instruments of human culture. But it was some time longer before I began to know this by personal experience. The only one of the imaginative arts in which I had from childhood taken great pleasure, was music; the best effect of which (and in this it surpasses perhaps every other art) consists in exciting enthusiasm; in winding up to a high pitch those feelings of an elevated kind which are already in the character, but to which this excitement gives a glow and a fervour, which, though transitory at its utmost height, is precious for sustaining them at other times. This effect of music I had often experienced; but like all my pleasurable susceptibilities it was suspended during the gloomy period. I had sought relief again and again from this quarter, but found none. After the tide had turned and I was in process of recovery, I had been helped forward by music, but in a much less elevated manner. I at this time first became acquainted with Weber's *Oberon*,° and the extreme pleasure which I drew from its delicious melodies did me good, by showing me a source of pleasure to which I was as susceptible as ever. The good, however, was much impaired by the thought, that the pleasure of music (as is quite true of such pleasure as this was, that of mere tune) fades with familiarity, and requires either to be revived by intermit-

---

°*Oberon:*   an opera performed in London in 1826

tence, or fed by continual novelty. And it is very characteristic both of my then state, and of the general tone of my mind at this period of my life, that I was seriously tormented by the thought of the exhaustibility of musical combinations. The octave consists only of five tones and two semitones, which can be put together in only a limited number of ways, of which but a small proportion are beautiful: most of these, it seemed to me, must have been already discovered, and there could not be room for a long succession of Mozarts and Webers, to strike out, as these had done, entirely new and surpassingly rich veins of musical beauty. This source of anxiety may, perhaps, be thought to resemble that of the philosophers of Laputa,° who feared lest the sun should be burnt out. It was, however, connected with the best feature in my character, and the only good point to be found in my very unromantic and in no way honourable distress. For though my dejection, honestly looked at, could not be called other than egotistical, produced by the ruin, as I thought, of my fabric of happiness, yet the destiny of mankind in general was ever in my thoughts, and could not be separated from my own. I felt that the flaw in my life must be a flaw in life itself; that the question was, whether, if the reformers of society and government could succeed in their objects, and every person in the community were free and in a state of physical comfort, the pleasures of life, being no longer kept up by struggle and privation, would cease to be pleasures. And I felt that unless I could see my way to some better hope than this for human happiness in general, my dejection must continue; but that if I could see such an outlet, I should then look on the world with pleasure; content as far as I was myself concerned, with any fair share of the general lot.

This state of my thoughts and feelings made the fact of my reading Wordsworth for the first time (in the autumn of 1828), an important event in my life. I took up the collection of his poems from curiosity, with no expectation of mental relief from it, though I had before resorted to poetry with that hope. In the worst period of my depression, I had read through the whole of Byron (then new to me), to try whether a poet, whose peculiar department was supposed to be that of the intenser feelings, could rouse any feeling in me. As might be expected, I got no good from this reading, but the reverse. The poet's state of mind was too like my own. His was the lament of a man who had worn out all pleasures, and who seemed to think that life, to all who possess the good things of it, must necessarily be the vapid, uninteresting thing which I found it. . . . But while Byron was exactly what did not suit my condition, Wordsworth was exactly what did. I had looked into *The Excursion* two or three years before, and found little in it; and I should probably have found as little had I read it at this time. But the miscellaneous poems, in the two-volume edition of 1815 (to which little of value was added in the latter part of the

---

°*Laputa:* in *Gulliver's Travels*

author's life), proved to be the precise thing for my mental wants at that particular juncture.

In the first place, these poems addressed themselves powerfully to one of the strongest of my pleasurable susceptibilities, the love of rural objects and natural scenery; to which I had been indebted not only for much of the pleasure of my life, but quite recently for relief from one of my longest relapses into depression. In this power of rural beauty over me, there was a foundation laid for taking pleasure in Wordsworth's poetry; the more so, as his scenery lies mostly among mountains, which, owing to my early Pyrenean excursion,° were my ideal of natural beauty. But Wordsworth would never have had any great effect on me, if he had merely placed before me beautiful pictures of natural scenery. Scott° does this still better than Wordsworth, and a very second-rate landscape does it more effectually than any poet. What made Wordsworth's poems a medicine for my state of mind, was that they expressed, not mere outward beauty, but states of feeling, and of thought coloured by feeling, under the excitement of beauty. They seemed to be the very culture of the feelings, which I was in quest of. In them I seemed to draw from a source of inward joy, of sympathetic and imaginative pleasure, which could be shared in by all human beings; which had no connexion with struggle or imperfection, but would be made richer by every improvement in the physical or social condition of mankind. From them I seemed to learn what would be the perennial sources of happiness, when all the greater evils of life shall have been removed. And I felt myself at once better and happier as I came under their influence. There have certainly been, even in our own age, greater poets than Wordsworth; but poetry of deeper and loftier feeling could not have done for me at that time what his did. I needed to be made to feel that there was real, permanent happiness in tranquil contemplation. Wordsworth taught me this, not only without turning away from, but with a greatly increased interest in the common feelings and common destiny of human beings. And the delight which these poems gave me, proved that with culture of this sort, there was nothing to dread from the most confirmed habit of analysis. At the conclusion of the Poems came the famous Ode, falsely called Platonic, "Intimations of Immortality": in which, along with more than his usual sweetness of melody and rhythm, and along with the two passages of grand imagery but bad philosophy so often quoted, I found that he too had had similar experience to mine; that he also had felt that the first freshness of youthful enjoyment of life was not lasting; but that he had sought for compensation, and found it, in the way in which he was now teaching me to find it. The result was that I gradually, but completely, emerged from my habitual depression, and was never again subject to it.

°*excursion:*   Mill had traveled to Spain and France in his youth and had visited the
  Pyrenees   °*Scott:*   Walter Scott, the novelist

*   *   *

Carlyle was a contemporary of Mill's, and the two are often usefully contrasted as representing equally sensitive but fundamentally different responses to problems of their time. Mill was brought up as a scientific rationalist and Utilitarian, Carlyle as a Scottish Presbyterian. Mill's writing is dry and logical, Carlyle's is colorful and dramatic. As an escape from the dark night of the soul, Mill recommends logical psychological procedures, Carlyle a statement of faith. But though they represent different temperaments and support different social and moral positions, they experience the problem in similar ways.

Carlyle's protagonist in *Sartor Resartus* is Diogenes Teufelsdröckh. The account of Teufelsdröckh's wanderings and spiritual biography are "told" by an "editor," who has assembled these records from bags of confused notes and scribbling. The story is a familiar one: the disillusionment of the young philosopher with conventional education, his loss of prospects for success, the rejection of his love by the beautiful Blumine in favor of his friend, and his casting forth into the world without money, hope, or prospects to nurse his psychological wounds and seek redemption.

From SARTOR RESARTUS

Thomas Carlyle (1795–1881)

THE EVERLASTING NO

Loss of Hope, and of Belief. Profit-and Loss Philosophy. Teufelsdröckh in his darkness and despair still clings to Truth and follows Duty. Inexpressible pains and fears of Unbelief. Fever-crisis: Protest against the Everlasting No: Baphometic° Fire-baptism.

Under the strange nebulous envelopment, wherein our Professor° has now shrouded himself, no doubt but his spiritual nature is nevertheless progressive, and growing: for how can the "Son of Time," in any case, stand still? We° behold him, through those dim years, in a state of crisis, of transition: his mad Pilgrimings, and general solution into aimless Discontinuity, what is all this but a mad Fermentation; wherefrom, the fiercer it is, the clearer product will one day evolve itself ?

°*Baphometic:* sudden or flame-like   °*our Professor:* Teufelsdröckh   °*We:* The hard-pressed editor, as opposed to "he" (Teufelsdröckh) or "I" (also Teufelsdröckh) in passages "quoted" from his writings by the editor.

Such transitions are ever full of pain: thus the Eagle when he moults is sickly, and, to attain his new beak, must harshly dash-off the old one upon rocks. What Stoicism soever our Wanderer° in his individual acts and motions, may affect, it is clear that there is a hot fever of anarchy and misery raging within; coruscations° of which flash out; as, indeed, how could there be other? Have we not seen him disappointed, bemocked of Destiny, through long years? All that the young heart might desire and pray for has been denied; nay, as in the last worst instance, offered and then snatched away.° Ever an "excellent Passivity"; but of useful, reasonable Activity, essential to the former as Food to Hunger, nothing granted: till at length, in this wild Pilgrimage, he must forcibly seize for himself an Activity, though useless, unreasonable. Alas, his cup of bitterness, which had been filling drop by drop, ever since that first "ruddy morning" in the Hinterschlag Gymnasium,° was at the very lip; and then with that poison-drop, of the Towgood-and-Blumine business,° it runs over, and even hisses over in a deluge of foam.

He himself says once, with more justice than originality: "Man is, properly speaking, based upon Hope, he has no other possession but Hope; this world of his is emphatically the "Place of Hope." What, then, was our Professor's possession? We see him, for the present, quite shut-out from Hope; looking not into the golden orient, but vaguely all round into a dim copper firmament, pregnant with earthquake and tornado.

Alas, shut-out from Hope, in a deeper sense than we yet dream of! For, as he wanders wearisomely through this world, he has now lost all tidings of another and higher. Full of religion, or at least of religiosity, as our Friend has since exhibited himself, he hides not that, in those days, he was wholly irreligious: "Doubt had darkened into Unbelief," says he; "shade after shade goes grimly over your soul, till you have the fixed, starless, Tartarean black." To such readers as have reflected, what can be called reflecting, on man's life, and happily discovered, in contradiction to much Profit-and-Loss Philosophy,° speculative and practical, that Soul is *not* synonymous with Stomach; who understand, therefore, in our Friend's words, "that, for man's well-being, Faith is properly the one thing needful; how, with it, Martyrs, otherwise weak, can cheerfully endure the shame and the cross; and without it, Worldlings puke-up their sick existence, by suicide, in the midst of luxury": to such it will be clear that, for a pure moral nature, the loss of his religious Belief was the loss of everything. Unhappy young man! All wounds, the crush of long-continued Destitution, the stab of false Friendship and of false Love, all wounds in thy so genial heart, would have healed again, had not its life-warmth been

---

°*Wanderer:* Teufelsdröckh   °*coruscations:* brilliant impulses   °*snatched away:* Blumine's pretense of love   °*Gymnasium:* where Teufelsdröckh began to be afflicted by the Spirit of Inquiry (a Gymnasium is a German secondary school) °*business:* her giving up Teufelsdröckh for Towgood   °*Profit-and-Loss Philosophy:* Utilitarianism, materialism

withdrawn. Well might he exclaim, in his wild way: "Is there no God, then; but at best an absentee God, sitting idle, ever since the first Sabbath, at the outside of his Universe, and *seeing* it go?° Has the word Duty no meaning; is what we call Duty no divine Messenger and Guide, but a false earthly Fantasm, made-up of Desire and Fear, of emanations from the Gallows and from Doctor Graham's Celestial-Bed?° Happiness of an approving Conscience! Did not Paul of Tarsus, whom admiring men have since named Saint, feel that *he* was "the chief of sinners"; and Nero of Rome, jocund in spirit (*Wohlgemuth*), spend much of his time in fiddling? Foolish Word-monger and Motive-grinder, who in thy Logic-mill hast an earthly mechanism for the Godlike itself, and wouldst fain grind me out Virtue from the husks of Pleasure,°—I tell thee, Nay! To the unregenerate Prometheus Vinctus of a man, is it ever the bitterest aggravation of his wretchedness that he is conscious of Virtue, that he feels himself the victim not of suffering only, but of injustice. What then? Is the heroic inspiration we name Virtue but some Passion; some bubble of the blood, bubbling in the direction others profit by? I know not: only this I know, If what thou namest Happiness be our true aim, then we are all astray. With Stupidity and sound Digestion man may front much. But what, in these dull unimaginative days, are the terrors of Conscience to diseases of the Liver! Not on Morality, but on Cookery, let us build our stronghold: there brandishing our frying-pan, as censer,° let us offer sweet incense to the Devil, and live at ease on the fat things *he* has provided for his Elect!"

Thus has the bewildered Wanderer to stand, as so many have done, shouting question after question into the Sibyl-cave of Destiny, and receive no Answer but an Echo. It is all a grim Desert, this once-fair world of his; wherein is heard only the howling of wild-beasts, or the shrieks of despairing, hate-filled men; and no Pillar of Cloud by day, and no Pillar of Fire by night, any longer guides the Pilgrim. To such length has the spirit of Inquiry carried him. "But what boots it (*was thut's*)?" cries he: "it is but the common lot in this era. Not having come to spiritual majority prior to the *Siecle de Louis Quinze*,° and not being born purely a Loghead (*Dummkopf*), thou hadst no other outlook. The whole world is, like thee, sold to Unbelief; their old Temples of the God-head, which for long years have not been rainproof, crumble down; and men ask now: where is the God-head; our eyes never saw him?"

Pitiful enough were it, for all these wild utterances, to call our Diogenes wicked. Unprofitable servants as we all are, perhaps at no era of

---

°*"Is . . . go"*: allusion to the 18th century deistic conception of God as an artificer who, having created the universe, then lost interest in its operation   °*Celestial-Bed*: a device supposed to cure sterility invented by a notorious quack doctor   °*earthly . . . pleasure*: another reference to Utilitarian methods of rational calculation of moral principles   °*censer*: the incense container used in religious ritual   °*Siecle de Louis Quinze*: ironic: the name of the age of Rationalism and religious skepticism

his life was he more decisively the Servant of Goodness, the Servant of God, than even now when doubting God's existence. "One circumstance I note," says he: "after all the nameless woe that Inquiry, which for me, what it is not always, was genuine Love of Truth, had wrought me, I nevertheless still loved Truth, and would bate no jot° of my allegiance to her. 'Truth!' I cried, 'though the Heavens crush me for following her: no Falsehood! though a whole celestial Lubberland° were the price of Apostasy.' In conduct it was the same. Had a divine Messenger from the clouds, or miraculous Handwriting on the wall, convincingly proclaimed to me *This thou shalt do,* with what passionate readiness, as I often thought, would I have done it, had it been leaping into the infernal Fire. Thus, in spite of all Motive-grinders, and Mechanical Profit-and-Loss Philosophies, with the sick ophthalmia and hallucination they had brought on, was the Infinite nature of Duty still dimly present to me: living without God in the world, of God's light I was not utterly bereft; if my as yet sealed eyes, with their unspeakable longing, could nowhere see Him, nevertheless in my heart He was present, and His heaven-written Law still stood legible and sacred there."

Meanwhile, under all these tribulations, and temporal and spiritual destitutions, what must the Wanderer, in his silent soul, have endured! "The painfullest feeling," writes he, "is that of your own Feebleness (*Unkraft*); ever, as the English Milton says, to be weak is the true misery. And yet of your Strength there is and can be no clear feeling, save by what you have prospered in, by what you have done. Between vague wavering Capability and fixed indubitable Performance, what a difference! A certain inarticulate Self-consciousness dwells dimly in us; which only our Works can render articulate and decisively discernible. Our Works are the mirror wherein the spirit first sees its natural lineaments. Hence, too, the folly of that impossible Precept, *Know thyself;*° till it be translated into this partially possible one, *Know what thou canst work at.*

"But for me, so strangely unprosperous had I been, the net-result of my Workings amounted as yet simply to—Nothing. How then could I believe in my Strength, when there was as yet no mirror to see it in? Ever did this agitating, yet, as I now perceive, quite frivolous question, remain to me insoluble: Hast thou a certain Faculty, a certain Worth, such even as the most have not; or art thou the completest Dullard of these modern times? Alas, the fearful Unbelief is unbelief in yourself, and how could I believe? Had not my first, last Faith in myself, when even to me the Heavens seemed laid open, and I dared to love, been all-too cruelly

---

°*bate no jot:* give up no part of   °*Lubberland:* land of Cockaigne, or of plenty   °*Know thyself:* a maxim attributed to Solon, Socrates, Thales, etc.; inscribed over the portico of the temple at Delphi. Carlyle objected to this maxim as leading to morbid self-analysis

belied? The speculative Mystery of Life grew ever more mysterious to me: neither in the practical Mystery had I made the slightest progress, but been everywhere buffeted, foiled, and contemptuously cast out. A feeble unit in the middle of a threatening Infinitude, I seemed to have nothing given me but eyes, whereby to discern my own wretchedness. Invisible yet impenetrable walls, as of Enchantment, divided me from all living: was there, in the wide world, any true bosom I could press trustfully to mine? O Heaven, No, there was none! I kept a lock upon my lips: why should I speak much with that shifting variety of so-called Friends, in whose withered, vain and too-hungry souls Friendship was but an incredible tradition? In such cases, your resource is to talk little, and that little mostly from the Newspapers. Now when I look back, it was a strange isolation I then lived in. The men and women around me, even speaking with me, were but Figures; I had, practically, forgotten that they were alive, that they were not merely automatic. In the midst of their crowded streets and assemblages, I walked solitary; and (except as it was my own heart, not another's, that I kept devouring) savage also, as the tiger in his jungle. Some comfort it would have been, could I, like a Faust, have fancied myself tempted and tormented of the Devil; for a Hell, as I imagine, without Life, though only diabolic Life, were more frightful: but in our age of Down-pulling and Disbelief, the very Devil has been pulled down, you cannot so much as believe in a Devil. To me the Universe was all void of Life, of Purpose, of Volition, even of Hostility: it was one huge, dead, immeasurable Steam-engine, rolling on, in its dead indifference, to grind me limb from limb. O, the vast, gloomy, solitary Golgotha,° and Mill of Death! Why was the Living banished thither companionless, conscious? Why, if there is no Devil; nay, unless the Devil is your God?"

A prey incessantly to such corrosions, might not, moreover, as the worst aggravation to them, the iron constitution even of a Teufelsdröckh threaten to fail? We conjecture that he has known sickness; and, in spite of his locomotive habits, perhaps sickness of the chronic sort. Hear this, for example: "How beautiful to die of broken-heart, on Paper! Quite another thing in practice; every window of your Feeling, even of your Intellect, as it were, begrimed and mud-bespattered, so that no pure ray can enter; a whole Drugshop in your inwards; the fordone soul drowning slowly in quagmires of Disgust!"

Putting all which external and internal miseries together, may we not find in the following sentences, quite in our Professor's still vein, significance enough? "From Suicide a certain aftershine (*Nachschein*) of Christianity withheld me: perhaps also a certain idolence of character; for, was not that a remedy I had at any time within reach? Often, however, was there a question present to me: Should some one now, at the turning of that corner, blow thee suddenly out of Space, into the other World, or

---

°*Golgotha:*   Hebrew: *gulgōleth*, skull; place of skulls; Calvary

other No-world, by pistol-shot,—how were it? On which ground, too, I often, in sea-storms and sieged cities and other death-scenes, exhibited an imperturbability, which passed, falsely enough, for courage." ,

"So had it lasted," concludes the Wanderer, "so had it lasted, as in bitter protracted Death-agony, through long years. The heart within me, unvisited by any heavenly dew-drop was smouldering in sulphurous, slow-consuming fire. Almost since earliest memory I had shed no tear; or once only when I, murmuring half-audibly, recited Faust's Death-song, that wild *Selig der den er im Siegesglanze findet* (Happy whom *he* finds in Battle's splendour), and thought that of this last Friend even I was not forsaken, that Destiny itself could not doom me not to die. Having no hope, neither had I any definite fear, were it of Man or of Devil: nay, I often felt as if it might be solacing, could the Arch-Devil himself, though in Tartarean terrors, but rise to me, that I might tell him a little of my mind. And yet, strangely enough, I lived in a continual, indefinite, pining fear; tremulous, pusillanimous, apprehensive of I knew not what; it seemed as if all things in the Heavens above and the Earth were but boundless jaws of a devouring monster, wherein I, Palpitating, waited to be devoured.

"Full of such humour, and perhaps the miserablest man in the whole French Capital or suburbs, was I, one sultry Dog-day, after much peram-bulation, toiling along the dirty little *Rue Saint-Thomas de l'Enfer*,° among civic rubbish enough, in a close atmosphere, and over pavements hot as Nebuchadnezzar's Furnace, whereby doubtless my spirits were little cheered; when, all at once, there rose a Thought in me, and I asked myself: 'What *art* thou afraid of? Wherefore, like a coward, dost thou forever pip and whimper, and go cowering and trembling? Despicable biped! what is the sum-total of the worst that lies before thee? Death? Well, Death; and say the pangs of Tophet too, and all that the Devil and Man may, will or can do against thee! Hast thou not a heart; canst thou not suffer whatsoever it be; and, as a Child of Freedom, though outcast, trample Tophet itself under thy feet, while it consumes thee? Let it come, then; I will meet it and defy it!' And as I so thought, there rushed like a stream of fire over my whole soul; and I shook base Fear away from me forever. I was strong, of unknown strength; a spirit, almost a god. Ever from that time, the temper of my misery was changed: not Fear or whining Sorrow was it, but Indignation and grim fire-eyed Defiance.

"Thus had the Everlasting No *(das ewige Nein)* pealed authoritatively through all the recesses of my Being, of my Me; and then was it that my whole Me stood up, in native God-created majesty, and with emphasis recorded its Protest. Such a Protest, the most important transaction in Life, may that same Indignation and Defiance, in a psychological point of

---

°*Rue Saint-Thomas de l'Enfer:* literally, Hell Street; St. Thomas was the doubting disciple.

view, be fitly called. The Everlasting No had said: 'Behold, thou art fatherless, outcast, and the Universe is mine' (the Devil's); to which my whole Me now made answer: 'I am not thine, but Free, and forever hate thee!'

"It is from this hour that I incline to date my Spiritual Newbirth, or Baphometic Fire-baptism; perhaps I directly thereupon began to be a Man."

* * *

The Shadow of Reason

Carlyle and Mill wrote their accounts of their youthful encounters with the analytic spirit of the age long after the events, and the fact of their recital of these dark moments testifies to their recovery. We see that to the Romantic this process requires a journey, a passage, a movement, a working through of these dark moments. Readers of Romantic poetry must also understand the causes of this darkness; without this knowledge they can have no understanding of the poetry.

These causes are stated powerfully and intensely by the poems in this section. All contain the special elements of the conditions described by Mill and Carlyle: loss of faith in traditional moral and intellectual values, loss of simplicity, loss of belief in natural joy and ease, loss of spontaneity, increase in analytic self-consciousness, the inability to relate easily to other people and to the natural world, an excess of morbid introspection, and a neurotic intellectualism. The speakers in the poems all represent victims of Romantic consciousness and have in common the condition of knowing what is wrong but being unable to do anything about it.

Blake's unique account of Romantic consciousness is one of the earliest and most complex of all perceptions of the historical and psychological processes involved. *The Book of Urizen* is the account of the growth of Reason (Urizen is pronounced "your reason") and the separation of this faculty from its previous unity with Imagination and Desire. No one was more certain than Blake that this separation was worthy of the dramatic and intense language of this poem, and Blake was able to escape the paralysis of self-consciousness by warning against it with great energy.

From THE BOOK OF URIZEN (Chapter I)

William Blake (1757–1827)

1

Lo, a shadow of horror is risen
In Eternity! Unknown, unprolific,
Self-clos'd, all-repelling: what Demon
Hath form'd this abominable void,
This soul-shudd'ring vacuum? Some said   5
"It is Urizen." But unknown, abstracted,
Brooding, secret, the dark power hid.

2

Times on times he divided & measur'd
Space by space in his ninefold darkness,
Unseen, unknown; changes appear'd   10
Like desolate mountains, rifted furious
By the black winds of perturbation.

3

For he strove in battles dire,
In unseen conflictions with shapes
Bred from his forsaken wilderness   15
Of beast, bird, fish, serpent & element,
Combustion, blast, vapour and cloud.

4

Dark, revolving in silent activity:
Unseen in tormenting passions:
An activity unknown and horrible,   20
A self-contemplating shadow,
In enormous labours occupied.

5

But Eternals beheld his vast forests;
Age on ages he lay, clos'd inknown,
Brooding shut in the deep; all avoid   25
The petrific, abominable chaos.

6

His cold horrors silent, dark Urizen
Prepar'd; his ten thousands of thunders,

Rang'd in gloom'd array, stretch out across
The dread world; & the rolling of wheels,   30
As of swelling seas, sound in his clouds,
In his hills of stor'd snows, in his mountains
Of hail & ice; voices of terror
Are heard, like thunders of autumn
When the cloud blazes over the harvests.   35

*   *   *

The following selections from the work of Matthew Arnold reflect a
more direct intellectual and psychological account of the conflict between
natural spontaneous feeling and the chilling shadow of Reason and self-
consciousness. For Arnold it is the inner person, the true self that is
hidden beneath social conventions and words, or it is the juxtaposition of
the rustic and old and simpler time with modernity and urbanity.
Thought, to these speakers, dwells on what is lost by thinking.

THE BURIED LIFE

Matthew Arnold (1822–1888)

Light flows our war of mocking words, and yet,
Behold, with tears mine eyes are wet!
I feel a nameless sadness o'er me roll.
Yes, yes, we know that we can jest,
We know, we know that we can smile!   5
But there's a something in this breast,
To which thy light words bring no rest,
And thy gay smiles no anodyne.°
Give me thy hand, and hush awhile,

And turn those limpid eyes on mine,   10
And let me read there, love!° thy inmost soul.

Alas! is even love too weak
To unlock the heart, and let it speak?
Are even lovers powerless to reveal
To one another what indeed they feel?   15

°*anodyne:* pain-killer   °*love:*   Although this is a typical Romantic soliloquy, it has
another, a "Love," as a listener.

I knew the mass of men conceal'd
Their thoughts, for fear that if reveal'd
They would by other men be met
With blank indifference, or with blame reproved;
I knew they lived and moved   20
Trick'd in disguises, alien to the rest
Of men, and alien to themselves—and yet
The same heart beats in every human breast!   ,

But we, my love!—doth a like spell benumb
Our hearts, our voices?—must we too be dumb?   25

Ah, well for us, if even we,
Even for a moment, can get free
Our heart, and have our lips unchain'd;
For that which seals them hath been deep-ordain'd!

Fate, which foresaw   30
How frivolous a baby man would be—
By what distractions he would be possess'd,
How he would pour himself in every strife,
And well-nigh change his own identity—
That it might keep from his capricious play   35
His genuine self, and force him to obey
Even in his own despite his being's law,
Bade through the deep recesses of our breast
The unregarded river of our life
Pursue with indiscernible flow its way;   40
And that we should not see
The buried stream, and seem to be
Eddying at large in blind uncertainty,
Though driving on with it eternally.

But often, in the world's most crowded streets,   45
But often, in the din of strife,
There rises an unspeakable desire
After the knowledge of our buried life;
A thirst to spend our fire and restless force
In tracking out our true, original course;   50
A longing to inquire
Into the mystery of this heart which beats
So wild, so deep in us—to know
Whence our lives come and where they go.

And many a man in his own breast then delves,   55
But deep enough, alas! none ever mines.

And we have been on many thousand lines,
And we have shown, on each, spirit and power;
But hardly have we, for one little hour,
Been on our own line, have we been ourselves— 60
Hardly had skill to utter one of all
The nameless feelings that course through our breast,
But they course on for ever unexpress'd.
And long we try in vain to speak and act
Our hidden self, and what we say and do 65
Is eloquent, is well—but 'tis not true!
And then we will no more be rack'd
With inward striving, and demand
Of all the thousand nothings of the hour
Their stupefying power; 70
Ah yes, and they benumb us at our call!
Yet still, from time to time, vague and forlorn,
From the soul's subterranean depth upborne
As from an infinitely distant land,
Come airs, and floating echoes, and convey 75
A melancholy into all our day.

Only—but this is rare—
When a beloved hand is laid in ours,
When, jaded with the rush and glare
Of the interminable hours, 80
Our eyes can in another's eyes read clear,
When our world-deafen'd ear
Is by the tones of a loved voice caress'd—
A bolt is shot back somewhere in our breast,
And a lost pulse of feeling stirs again. 85
The eye sinks inward, and the heart lies plain,
And what we mean, we say, and what we would, we know.
A man becomes aware of his life's flow,
And hears its winding murmur; and he sees
The meadows where it glides, the sun, the breeze. 90

And there arrives a lull in the hot race
Wherein he doth for ever chase
That flying and elusive shadow, rest.
An air of coolness plays upon his face,
And an unwonted calm pervades his breast. 95
And then he thinks he knows
The hills where his life rose,
And the sea where it goes.

From THE SCHOLAR–GYPSY

Matthew Arnold

O born in days when wits were fresh and clear,
    And life ran gaily as the sparkling Thames;
      Before this strange disease of modern life,
    With its sick hurry, its divided aims,
      Its heads o'ertax'd, its palsied hearts, was rife—   5
      Fly hence, our contact fear!—
Still fly, plunge deeper in the bowering wood!
    Averse, as Dido did with gesture stern
    From her false friend's approach in Hades turn,°
Wave us away, and keep thy solitude!   10

Still nursing the unconquerable hope,
    Still clutching the inviolable shade,
      With a free, onward impulse brushing through,
    By night, the silver'd branches of the glade—
      Far on the forest-skirts, where none pursue.   15
      On some mild pastoral slope
Emerge, and resting on the moonlit pales°
    Freshen thy flowers as in former years
    With dew, or listen with enchanted ears,
From the dark dingles,° to the nightingales!   20

But fly our paths, our feverish contact fly!
    For strong the infection of our mental strife,
      Which, though it gives no bliss, yet spoils for rest;
    And we should win thee from thy own fair life,
      Like us distracted, and like us unblest.   25
      Soon, soon thy cheer would die,
Thy hopes grow timorous, and unfix'd thy powers,
    And thy clear aims be cross and shifting made;
    And then thy glad perennial youth would fade,
Fade, and grow old at last, and die like ours.   30

Then fly our greetings, fly our speech and smiles!
    —As some grave Tyrian° trader, from the sea,
      Descried at sunrise an emerging prow

°*Dido,* who had killed herself when Aeneas deserted her, turned away from him scornfully when he visited Hades.   °*pales:* fenceposts   °*dingles:* woods °*Tyrian trader:* a merchant from the Phoenician city of Tyre seeing the arrival of the "merry" Greek, carrying a new, less sensitive, more aggressive and conscious civilization

Lifting the cool-hair'd creepers stealthily,
    The fringes of a southward-facing brow   35
        Among the Ægæan isles;
And saw the merry Grecian coaster come,
    Freighted with amber grapes, and Chian wine,
    Green, bursting figs, and tunnies steeped in brine—
And knew the intruders on his ancient home,   40

The young light-hearted masters of the waves—
    And snatch'd his rudder, and shook out more sail;
    And day and night held on indignantly
O'er the blue Midland waters with the gale,
    Betwixt the Syrtes° and soft Sicily,   45
        To where the Atlantic raves
Outside the western straits;° and unbent sails
    There, where down cloudy cliffs, through sheets of foam,
    Shy traffickers, the dark Iberians° come;
And on the beach undid his corded bales.   50

From EMPEDOCLES ON ETNA

Matthew Arnold

Oh, that I could glow like this mountain!
Oh, that my heart bounded with the swell of sea!
Oh, that my soul were full of light as the stars!
Oh, that it brooded over the world like the air!

But no, this heart will glow no more; thou art   5
A living man no more, Empedocles!°
Nothing but a devouring flame of thought—
But a naked, eternally restless mind!
          After a pause: —

To the elements it came from
Everything will return   10
Our bodies to earth,
Our blood to water,

°*Syrtes:* Sidra on the northern coast of Africa °*straits:* Gibraltar
°*Iberians:* early inhabitants of Iberia (Spain). Arnold's point is to contrast the
simpler, more honest Phoenician trader with the Greek, and to recommend that the
Phoenician, like his Scholar–Gypsy, flee any contact with them, sailing away to Iberia
to find a proper place to do business.   °*Empedocles on Etna:* The philosopher
soliloquizes on the edge of the crater.

Heat to fire,
Breath to air.
They were well born, they will be well entomb'd— 15
But mind? . . .

And we might gladly share the fruitful stir
Down in our mother earth's miraculous womb;
Well would it be
With what roll'd of us in the stormy main; 20
We might have joy, blent with the all-bathing air,
Or with the nimble, radiant life of fire.

But mind—but thought—
If these have been the master part of us—
Where will *they* find their parent element? 25
What will receive *them*, who will call *them* home?
But we shall still be in them, and they in us.
And we shall be the strangers of the world,
And they will be our lords, as they are now;
And keep us prisoners of our consciousness, 30
And never let us clasp and feel the All
But through their forms, and modes, and stifling veils.
And we shall be unsatisfied as now;
And we shall feel the agony of thirst,
The ineffable longing for the life of life 35
Baffled for ever; and still thought and mind
Will hurry us with them on their homeless march,
Over the unallied unopening earth,
Over the unrecognising sea; while air
Will blow us fiercely back to sea and earth, 40
And fire repel us from its living waves.
And then we shall unwillingly return
Back to this meadow of calamity,
This uncongenial place, this human life;
And in our individual human state 45
Go through the sad probation all again,
To see if we will poise our life at last,
To see if we will now at last be true
To our own only true, deep-buried selves,
Being one with which we are one with the whole world; 50
Or whether we will once more fall away
Into some bondage of the flesh or mind,
Some slough of sense, or some fantastic maze
Forged by the imperious lonely thinking-power.
And each succeeding age in which we are born 55

Will have more peril for us than the last;
Will goad our senses with a sharper spur,
Will fret our minds to an intenser play,
Will make ourselves harder to be discern'd.
And we shall struggle awhile, gasp and rebel—   60
And we shall fly for refuge to past times,
Their soul of unworn youth, their breath of greatness;
And the reality will pluck us back,
Knead us in its hot hand, and change our nature
And we shall feel our powers of effort flag,   65
And rally them for one last fight—and fail;
And we shall sink in the impossible strife,
And be astray for ever.

                   Slave of sense
I have in no wise been; —but slave of thought? . . .   70
And who can say: I have been always free,
Lived ever in the light of my own soul?—
I cannot; I have lived in wrath and gloom,
Fierce, disputatious, ever at war with man,
Far from my own soul, far from warmth and light.   75
But I have not grown easy in these bonds—
But I have not denied what bonds these were.
Yea, I take myself to witness,
That I have loved no darkness,
Sophisticated no truth,   80
Nursed no delusion,
Allow'd no fear!

   And therefore, O ye elements! I know—
Ye know it too—it hath been granted me
Not to die wholly, not to be all enslaved.   85
I feel it in this hour. The numbing cloud
Mounts off my soul; I feel it, I breathe free.

Is it but for a moment?
    —Ah, boil up, ye vapours!
Leap and roar, thou sea of fire!   90
My soul glows to meet you.
Ere it flag, ere the mists
Of despondency and gloom
Rush over it again,
Receive me, save me!   95
          He plunges into the crater.

      *   *   *

In the following selection, Tennyson echoes the same concerns as Arnold: that in older, simpler days thought and speech were closer, and emotions went naturally and easily into action. But in the modern world, says Tennyson, we face an inevitable descent into despair and self-consciousness. Isolation comes upon the Self as it gains knowledge.

From IN MEMORIAM

Alfred, Lord Tennyson (1809–1892)

XXIII

Now, sometimes in my sorrow shut,
  Or breaking into song by fits,
  Alone, alone to where he sits,
The Shadow° cloaked from head to foot,

Who keeps the keys of all the creeds,   5
  I wander, often falling lame,
  And looking back to whence I came,
Or on to where the pathway leads;

And crying, How changed from where it ran
  Thro' lands where not a leaf was dumb,   10
  But all the lavish hills would hum
The murmur of a happy Pan;

When each by turns was guide to each,
  And Fancy light from Fancy caught,
  And Thought leapt out to wed with Thought   15
Ere Thought could wed itself with Speech;

And all we met was fair and good,
  And all was good that Time could bring,
  And all the secret of the Spring
Moved in the chambers of the blood;   20

And many an old philosophy
  On Argive° heights divinely sang,
  And round us all the thicket rang
To many a flute of Arcady.°

°*Shadow:* death   °*Argive:* Greek   °*Arcady:* rural, pastoral Greece

The baby new to earth and sky,   25
   What time his tender palm is prest
   Against the circle of the breast,
Has never thought that "this is I";

But as he grows he gathers much,
   And learns the use of "I" and "me,"   30
   And finds "I am not what I see,
And other than the things I touch."

So rounds he to a separate mind
   From whence clear memory may begin,
   As thro' the frame that binds him in   35
His isolation grows defined.

This use may lie in blood and breath,
   Which else were fruitless of their due,
   Had man to learn himself anew
Beyond the second birth of death.   40

*   *   *

Three Victims

The character of Hamlet exemplifies the state of isolated, emotionless self-consciousness, in which every emotion is immediately flawed and contradicted by thought, in which the impulse to act is crossed by second—and third and fourth—thoughts, by doubts, qualifications, and always, by talk and talk and talk. Hamlet's characteristic problem was recognized by sympathetic Romantic critics. In Hamlet's words, "the native hue of resolution / Is sicklied o'er with the pale cast of thought, / And enterprises of great pitch and moment / With this regard their currents turn awry, / And lose the name of action." It was because Coleridge saw much of his own problem and of Romantic psychological dilemmas in Hamlet that his account of the character remains the basis of most readings of the play and of the continuing interest in the character.

THE CHARACTER OF HAMLET

Samuel Taylor Coleridge (1772–1834)

Shakespeare's mode of conceiving characters [is] out of his own intellectual and moral faculties, by conceiving any one intellectual or moral faculty in morbid excess and then placing himself, thus mutilated and diseased, under given circumstances. This we shall have repeated occasion to restate and enforce. In Hamlet I conceive him to have wished to exemplify the moral necessity of a due balance between our attention to outward objects and our meditation on inward thoughts—a due balance between the real and the imaginary world. In Hamlet this balance does not exist—his thoughts, images, and fancy being far more vivid than his perceptions, and his very perceptions instantly passing thro' the medium of his contemplations, and acquiring as they pass a form and color not naturally their own. Hence great, enormous, intellectual activity, and a consequent proportionate aversion to real action, with all its symptoms and accompanying qualities. . . .

The first words that Hamlet speaks—

A little more than kin, and less than kind.

He begins with that play of words, the complete absence of which characterizes Macbeth. No one can have heard quarrels among the vulgar but must have noticed the close connection of punning with angry contempt. Add too what is highly characteristic of superfluous activity of mind, a sort of playing with a thread or watch chain or snuff box.

And note how the character develops itself in the next speech—the aversion to externals, the betrayed habit of brooding over the world within him, and the prodigality of beautiful words, which are, as it were, the half embodyings of thoughts, that make them more than thoughts, give them an outness, a reality *sui generis*, and yet retain their correspondence and shadowy approach to the images and movements within.

The first soliloquy: "O that this too too solid flesh would melt . . ." The reasons why *taedium vitae* oppresses minds like Hamlet's: the exhaustion of bodily feeling from perpetual exertion of mind; that all mental form being indefinite and ideal, realities must needs become cold, and hence it is the indefinite that combines with passion. . . .

Hamlet's running into long reasonings while waiting for the ghost, carrying off the impatience and uneasy feelings of expectation by running away from the *particular* into the *general*. This aversion to personal, individual concerns, and escape to generalizations and general reasonings [is] a most important characteristic.

. . . What then was the point to which Shakespeare directed himself in Hamlet? He intended to portray a person in whose view the external world and all its incidents and objects were comparatively dim and of no interest in themselves, and which began to interest only when they were reflected in the mirror of his mind. Hamlet beheld external things in the same way that a man of vivid imagination who shuts his eyes sees what has previously made an impression on his organs.

*　　*　　*

The title of the following poem by Tennyson refers to the heroine of Shakespeare's play *Measure for Measure* but without special reference to the play. The idea is to dramatize alienation, that state of mind in which the causes of depression are known well enough by the sufferer who, however, remains powerless to act to relieve the symptoms or condition. The imagery that surrounds the unhappy woman—empty rooms, solitary landscape, isolation—is typical of the symbolism of this state of mind.

MARIANA

Alfred, Lord Tennyson (1809–1892)

> "Mariana in the moated grange."
> *Measure for Measure*

With blackest moss the flower-plots
　　Were thickly crusted, one and all;
The rusted nails fell from the knots
　　That held the pear to the gable-wall.
The broken sheds look'd sad and strange:　　　5
　　Uplifted was the clinking latch;
　　Weeded and worn the ancient thatch
Upon the lonely moated grange.
　　　She only said, "My life is dreary,
　　　　He cometh not," she said;　　　10
　　　She said, "I am aweary, aweary,
　　　　I would that I were dead!"

Her tears fell with the dews at even;
　　Her tears fell ere the dews were dried;
She could not look on the sweet heaven,　　　15
　　Either at morn or eventide.
After the flitting of the bats,
　　When thickest dark did trance the sky,

She drew her casement-curtain by,
And glanced athwart the glooming flats, 20
    She only said, "The night is dreary,
      He cometh not," she said;
    She said, "I am aweary, aweary,
      I would that I were dead!"

Upon the middle of the night, 25
    Waking she heard the night-fowl crow;
The cock sung out an hour ere light;
    From the dark fen the oxen's low
Came to her; without hope of change,
    In sleep she seem'd to walk forlorn, 30
Till cold winds woke the gray-eyed morn
About the lonely moated grange.
    She only said, "The day is dreary,
      He cometh not," she said;
    She said, "I am aweary, aweary, 35
      I would that I were dead!"

About a stone-cast from the wall
    A sluice with blacken'd waters slept,
And o'er it many, round and small,
    The cluster'd marish-mosses crept. 40
Hard by a poplar shook alway,
    All silver-green with gnarled bark:
For leagues no other tree did mark
The level waste, the rounding gray.
    She only said, "My life is dreary, 45
      He cometh not," she said;
    She said, "I am aweary, aweary.
      I would that I were dead!"

And ever when the moon was low,
    And the shrill winds were up and away, 50
In the white curtain, to and fro,
    She saw the gusty shadow sway.
But when the moon was very low,
    And wild winds bound within their cell,
The shadow of the poplar fell 55
Upon her bed, across her brow.
    She only said, "The night is dreary,
      He cometh not," she said;
    She said, "I am aweary, aweary,
      I would that I were dead!" 60

All day within the dreamy house,
   The doors upon their hinges creak'd;
The blue fly sung in the pane; the mouse
   Behind the mouldering wainscot shriek'd,
Or from the crevice peer'd about.   65
     Old faces glimmer'd thro' the doors,
     Old footsteps trod the upper floors,
   Old voices called her from without.
       She only said, "My life is dreary,
         He cometh not," she said;   70
       She said, "I am aweary, aweary,
         I would that I were dead!"

The sparrow's chirrup on the roof,
   The slow clock ticking, and the sound
Which to the wooing wind aloof   75
   The poplar made, did all confound
Her sense; but most she loathed the hour
   When the thick-moted sunbeam lay
   Athwart the chambers, and the day
Was sloping toward his western bower.   80
     Then said she, "I am very dreary,
       He will not come," she said;
     She wept, "I am aweary, aweary,
       O God, that I were dead!"

          *   *   *

    The next poem gives the soliloquy of a less heroic figure: The speaker knows certainly that he is not Hamlet. He is a man whose self-consciousness is acute and painful, even though it is compounded of essentially trivial things. It is society now—manners, conventions, teas and cakes and ices, and gossipy women and his own concerns lest they judge him adversely—that place Prufrock in his resigned pathetic circumstance. Though he thinks of greatness—Hamlet, John the Baptist, Lazarus—though he contemplates natural and sensual energy—sea-girls and perfume—he knows that all visions have revisions, that the momentous questions will never be asked, that he has accepted his condition, and that his love song is pitiable and weak.

THE LOVE SONG OF J. ALFRED PRUFROCK

T. S. Eliot (1888–1965)

> *S'io credesse che mia risposta fosse*
> *A persona che mai tornasse al mondo,*
> *Questa fiamma staria senza piu scosse.*
> *Ma perciocche giammai di questo fondo*
> *Non torno vivo alcun, s'i'odo il vero,*
> *Senza tema d'infamia ti rispondo.*°

Let us go then, you and I,
When the evening is spread out against the sky
Like a patient etherised upon a table;
Let us go, through certain half-deserted streets,
The muttering retreats   5
Of restless nights in one-night cheap hotels
And sawdust restaurants with oyster-shells:
Streets that follow like a tedious argument
Of insidious intent
To lead you to an overwhelming question . . .   10
Oh, do not ask, "What is it?"
Let us go and make our visit.

In the room the women come and go
Talking of Michelangelo.

The yellow fog that rubs its back upon the window-panes,   15
The yellow smoke that rubs its muzzle on the window-panes
Licked its tongue into the corners of the evening,
Lingered upon the pools that stand in drains,
Let fall upon its back the soot that falls from chimneys,
Slipped by the terrace, made a sudden leap,   20
And seeing that it was a soft October night,
Curled once about the house, and fell asleep.

And indeed there will be time
For the yellow smoke that slides along the street,
Rubbing its back upon the window-panes;   25

°The epigram is from Dante's *Inferno*; it is the statement of one of the lost souls who, speaking to Dante and Virgil, says that he can speak freely since he knows that none who venture that far into Hell can ever return to earth.

There will be time, there will be time
To prepare a face to meet the faces that you meet;
There will be time to murder and create,
And time for all the works and days of hands
That lift and drop a question on your plate;   30
Time for you and time for me,
And time yet for a hundred indecisions,
And for a hundred visions and revisions,
Before the taking of a toast and tea.

    In the room the women come and go   35
Talking of Michelangelo.

    And indeed there will be time
To wonder, "Do I dare?" and, "Do I dare?"
Time to turn back and descend the stair,
With a bald spot in the middle of my hair—   40
[They will say: "How his hair is growing thin!"]
My morning coat, my collar mounting firmly to the chin,
My necktie rich and modest, but asserted by a simple pin—
[They will say: "But how his arms and legs are thin!"]
Do I dare   45
Disturb the universe?
In a minute there is time
For decisions and revisions which a minute will reverse.

    For I have known them all already, known them all:—
Have known the evenings, mornings, afternoons,   50
I have measured out my life with coffee spoons;
I know the voices dying with a dying fall
Beneath the music from a farther room.
    So how should I presume?

    And I have known the eyes already, known them all—   55
The eyes that fix you in a formulated phrase,
And when I am formulated, sprawling on a pin,
When I am pinned and wriggling on the wall,
Then how should I begin
To spit out all the butt-ends of my days and ways?   60
    And how should I presume?

    And I have known the arms already, known them all—
Arms that are braceleted and white and bare
[But in the lamplight, downed with light brown hair!]
Is it perfume from a dress   65

That makes me so digress?
Arms that lie along a table, or wrap about a shawl.
    And should I then presume?
    And how should I begin?

. . . . .

Shall I say, I have gone at dusk through narrow streets   70
And watched the smoke that rises from the pipes
Of lonely men in shirt-sleeves, leaning out of windows? . . .

    I should have been a pair of ragged claws
Scuttling across the floors of silent seas.

. . . . .

And the afternoon, the evening, sleeps so peacefully!   75
Smoothed by long fingers,
Asleep . . . tired . . . or it malingers,
Stretched on the floor, here beside you and me.
Should I, after tea and cakes and ices,
Have the strength to force the moment to its crisis?   80
But though I have wept and fasted, wept and prayed,
Though I have seen my head [grown slightly bald] brought in
        upon a platter,
I am no prophet—and here's no great matter;
I have seen the moment of my greatness flicker,
And I have seen the eternal Footman hold my coat, and snicker,   85
And in short, I was afraid.

    And would it have been worth it, after all,
After the cups, the marmalade, the tea,
Among the porcelain, among some talk of you and me,
Would it have been worth while,   90
To have bitten off the matter with a smile,
To have squeezed the universe into a ball
To roll it toward some overwhelming question,
To say: "I am Lazarus, come from the dead,
Come back to tell you all, I shall tell you all"—   95
If one, settling a pillow by her head,
    Should say: "That is not what I meant at all.
    That is not it, at all."

    And would it have been worth it, after all,
Would it have been worth while,   100

After the sunsets and the dooryards and the sprinkled streets,
After the novels, after the teacups, after the skirts that trail along
    the floor—
And this, and so much more?—
It is impossible to say just what I mean!
But as if a magic lantern threw the nerves in patterns on a screen: 105
Would it have been worth while
If one, settling a pillow or throwing off a shawl,
And turning toward the window, should say:
    "That is not it at all,
    That is not what I meant, at all."   110

. . . . .

No! I am not Prince Hamlet, nor was meant to be;
Am an attendant lord, one that will do
To swell a progress, start a scene or two,
Advise the prince; no doubt, an easy tool,
Deferential, glad to be of use,   115
Politic, cautious, and meticulous;
Full of high sentence, but a bit obtuse;
At times, indeed, almost ridiculous—
Almost, at times, the Fool.

    I grow old . . . I grow old . . .   120
I shall wear the bottoms of my trousers rolled.

    Shall I part my hair behind? Do I dare to eat a peach?
I shall wear white flannel trousers, and walk upon the beach.
I have heard the mermaids singing, each to each.

    I do not think that they will sing to me.   125

    I have seen them riding seaward on the waves
Combing the white hair of the waves blown back
When the wind blows the water white and black.

    We have lingered in the chambers of the sea
By sea-girls wreathed with seaweed red and brown   130
Till human voices wake us, and we drown.

*   *   *

QUESTIONS

1. Why, in Mill's view, was the associational theory of education inadequate?
2. Marmontel's account of his father's death is not a particularly moving passage, yet its effect on Mill was decisive. What can account for this fact? What aspects of Mill's situation seem unclear or to need further explanation?
3. What is Mill's remedy for excessive self-consciousness?
4. Mill argues that his depression was important not only for the personal element, that the problem was not only a "flaw in my life," but "a flaw in life itself." Why does he see it as such, and to what extent does this seem a valid opinion?
5. Why do music and scenery seem particularly important to Mill as a remedy for depression?
6. Nature and natural scenes and objects play important parts in Romantic psychology. Why does Mill value these aspects of experience?
7. What was the fundamental cause of Teufelsdröckh's condition? Why was his condition more serious than discouragement with worldly prospects?
8. Notice that Mill in referring to the passage from Coleridge also refers to the loss of Hope as a fundamental condition of this state of mind. What does Hope usually provide for man?
9. "Profit-and-Loss Philosophy" holds that Soul is synonymous with Stomach. Why is Carlyle opposed to such a view? Why does such a view contribute to "Worldlings" puking up their sick existence? How does such a philosophy occur? What are its fundamental assumptions?
10. Explain how "the spirit of Inquiry" carries Teufelsdröckh into the "grim Desert." What part of Mill's account corresponds to this description? What other metaphors are used to describe Teufelsdröckh's depressed state of mind?
11. What realization begins Teufelsdröckh's recovery? In his solitude, what idea begins to turn him from despair?
12. Why does not Reason offer Teufelsdröckh a means for Hope?
13. Mill and Carlyle are writing of the same psychological condition and experience but in very different manners. What are the strengths and weaknesses of each manner?
14. Urizen is described as "unknown, unprolific, self-clos'd, all-repelling." Explain these terms. How do they apply to the Romantic idea of reason?
15. Where and in what condition has Urizen been? Discuss the idea of reason as "rising" after ages of concealment.
16. The contrast between the present and some vision of better, older days is a common one, and most historical periods have had people

who saw the losses resulting from their modernity. What particular virtues does Arnold see as missing from his contemporary age, and what particular pains and problems ensue from these losses?

17. What does the absence in these poems of any other speaker do to account for the speaker's condition? Construct a dialogue between them and listeners. What remedies to their situation do they seem to be missing? To what extent does their selfhood offer the possibility of redemption? What strengths do they have?

18. Comment on the strengths and weaknesses of the use of Reason. What validity is there in the Romantic opposition to Reason, Analysis, and Science? What faculty do we think of as the opposite of Reason? What are its strengths and weaknesses? What aspects of modern life lend their support to Reason? What to other faculties and powers?

19. What light is cast on Hamlet's character by Romantic theories of the dark night of the soul? To what extent is he a victim of blighted prospects, of disillusionment, of too much reason?

20. Hamlet and Mariana both consider suicide. Explain the circumstances that bring them to this state of mind. Compare these accounts with those offered by Mill and Carlyle. Why is suicide the rejection of Romanticism?

21. What difference does the dark night of the soul have when it occurs in the mind of a woman?

22. Prufrock is a more modern sufferer. Compare his problem with those of Hamlet and Mariana. What does Prufrock think of Hamlet? Why? What are the important images that reflect Profrock's suffering and isolation?

23. Which of the three victims seems to be the most sympathetic, the most sensitive to the problem?

PART IV

Redemption

Redemption

Analysis, elaboration, and expression of the state of depression, painful as it may be, has in Romantic psychology a necessary purpose and is not an end in itself. Only in certain morbid sicknesses does Romantic consciousness dramatize its pain without looking forward to relief. The idea of aspiration, of movement and development that we have discussed earlier applies to the Self. Thus, a full experience of the dark night of the soul may be preparation for change, for a movement out of paralysis toward the assertion or reassertion of the creative, loving powers.

Belief in this possibility of redemption is derived from a fundamental axiom of the Romantic point of view: that the Self, or Soul, or Will contains, or can acquire, sufficient energy or power to recover from states of self-consciousness and alienation. Human consciousness contains an inherent strength or energy, called variously Imagination, Creative Will, or more simply, Love, Joy, or Sympathy. In even the darkest hour this power is always latent, always offering the possibility of throwing off alienation, doubt, despair, and negative states of consciousness. Redemption, therefore, is the assertion of these inner powers, the recognition of a vital Self-Energy, which allows creativity and affirmation.

(This idea has received considerable publicity in current movements in popular psychology which emphasize self-assertion, positive thinking, and the development of "human potential." In some ways it anticipates the more serious and well-developed branch of psychotherapy described generally as ego psychology. It may be contrasted also in a useful way with the traditional Christian view in which suffering and despair are related to a state of sin and to a fall from Grace. Redemption from these states can occur only by authority of some external power, usually God's grace and mercy, which is offered only on the condition of the Submission of the Self to these Outside Powers and Forms. The method is confession, contrition, and humility, the abnegation of Self.)

Redemption is marked by a variety of symptoms and attitudes, but most fundamental and typical is that the Self becomes capable of producing and experiencing affirmative, sympathetic feelings toward the objects of the external world, and especially toward other people, other Selves, and toward the living creatures of nature. Since perception is an act of projection of the Self, people and things are "dead" or "alive" depending on the way they are viewed. In a state of depression the objects and people are dead, that is, mechanical, unconnected, objectified, and distant, seen without feeling. Redemption allows the Self to find in itself the power to view things and people differently, to see them as connected, related to one another and to the viewer. The Self becomes as a lamp, as an illuminator, and things that were dead take on a power, vitality, and interest.

Though this idea is difficult to state simply, it is asserted in many of the great Romantic poems, which are in effect testimonies to faith in this power. Moreover, these poems assert not only that the Self can generate its own Redemption but that it can enact the very process itself, enlisting the reader's sympathy and participation in the process. This "poetry of experience," as Langbaum° has called it, shows the movement from one psychological condition to another, and the process of reading the poem carefully offers readers an opportunity, so to speak, for a redemption of their own, as they see into the consciousness and hear the voice of the poem.

Not all poems achieve this final state of redemption. Sometimes they lead to further doubts and questions, or to a tension between one state of mind and another, or to a confrontation between two ideas or conditions. The conclusion is not as significant as the process by which feelings have been generated or as the signs of life and creativity the encounter has produced. When feelings are engaged, they show that the Outside world has been engaged, that Isolation, Self-Consciousness, and Solitude have been overcome. What we look for, then, is not an answer, not some belief adopted, not some new faith in something external. What we look for in these poems is evidence of the Self making something, enacting or achieving sympathies with others and other things, feeling relationships with the external world, entering upon a psychological reciprocity with Nature or with Humanity. Evidence of the Will to do this, however hesitant or brief, is evidence of Redemption and represents the fundamental faith in a world created in love by the Self, by the Self freed from reason, science, analysis, and doubt, freed to use its own powers for redemptive purposes.

*   *   *

A number of metaphors express the engagement between the Self and the World. As mentioned earlier, vision may be seen as a projection of some light or power out of the Self into the world. Or this power may be a fountain overflowing, a wind sweeping over a dead landscape bringing it to life, even an erotic impregnator of sterile matter. Whitman's list of people, places, and things in *Song of Myself* that are "part of himself" is another pattern for this act. In the following poem, he employs a simple figure for the way in which the Self, isolated and alone, faces and confronts the vast, inert, lifeless Space in which it finds itself.

°See Part V.

A NOISELESS PATIENT SPIDER

Walt Whitman (1819–1892)

A noiseless patient spider,
I mark'd where on a little promontory it stood isolated,
Mark'd how to explore the vacant vast surrounding,
It launch'd forth filament, filament, filament, out of itself,
Ever unreeling them, ever tirelessly speeding them.   5

And you O my soul where you stand,
Surrounded, detached, in measureless oceans of space,
Ceaselessly musing, venturing, throwing, seeking the spheres to connect
    them,
Till the bridge you will need be form'd, till the ductile anchor hold,
Till the gossamer thread you fling catch somewhere, O my soul.   10

*   *   *

The following poem, like those given later by Keats, Shelley, Wordsworth, and Yeats, is a typical Romantic lyric, a poem of experience, in which a psychological process is enacted as the poem unfolds. Such poems require careful and detailed study. They are condensed and contain a variety of complex psychological circumstances in a short space. They commonly carry out abstract or mental attitudes metaphorically, and they try to enlist the reader's participation in the experience being described. All of them use the same general pattern: A state of dejection or despair is described, various remedies and escapes are discussed or suggested, and a new state of awareness—better, deeper, more humane and productive than the condition with which the poem began—is reached. Although it is neither the greatest nor the clearest poem of this type, *Dejection* does work through the typical process carefully and exactly, giving a history of the problem and speculations about the ways in which "Joy," as Coleridge calls it, may be known.

DEJECTION: AN ODE

Samuel Taylor Coleridge (1772–1836)

> *Late, late yestreen I saw the new Moon,*
> *With the old Moon in her arms;*
> *And I fear, I fear, my Master dear!*
> *We shall have a deadly storm.*
>
> Ballad, Sir Patrick Spence

I

Well! If the Bard was weather-wise, who made
   The grand old ballad of Sir Patrick Spence, — *Calm*
   This night, so tranquil now, will not go hence
Unroused by winds, that ply a busier trade
Than those which mould yon cloud in lazy flakes,   5
Or the dull sobbing draft, that moans and rakes
Upon the strings of this Æolian lute,°
   Which better far were mute.
   For lo! the New-moon winter-bright!
   And overspread with phantom light,   10
   (With swimming phantom light o'erspread
   But rimmed and circled by a silver thread)
I see the old Moon in her lap, foretelling
   The coming-on of rain and squally blast.
And oh! that even now the gust were swelling, — *Picking up.* 15
   And the slant night-shower driving loud and fast!
Those sounds which oft have raised me, whilst they awed,
   And sent my soul abroad,
Might now perhaps their wonted impulse give,
Might startle this dull pain, and make it moved and live!   20

II

A grief without a pang, void, dark, and drear,
   A stifled, drowsy, unimpassioned grief,
   Which finds no natural outlet, no relief,
     In word, or sigh, or tear—
O Lady!° in this wan and heartless mood,   25
To other thoughts by yonder throstle woo'd,
   All this long eve, so balmy and serene,

°*Aeolian lute:* a wind-harp, set in a window and stirred to music by the wind; a favorite metaphor of Romantic poetry to suggest among other things harmony between man and Nature   °*Lady:* Sara Hutchinson, Wordsworth's sister-in-law

Have I been gazing on the western sky,
    And its peculiar tint of yellow green:
And still I gaze—and with now blank an eye!   30
And those thin clouds above, in flakes and bars,
That give away their motion to the stars;
Those stars, that glide behind them or between,
Now sparkling, now bedimmed, but always seen:
You crescent Moon, as fixed as if it grew   35
In its own cloudless, starless lake of blue;
I see them all so excellently fair,
I see, not feel, how beautiful they are!

III

    My genial spirits fail;
    And what can these avail   40
To lift the smothering weight from off my breast?
        It were a vain endeavour,
        Though I should gaze for ever
On that green light that lingers in the west:
I may not hope from outward forms to win   45
The passion and the life, whose fountains are within.

IV

O Lady! we receive but what we give,
And in our life alone does Nature live:
Ours° is her wedding garment, ours her shroud!
    And would we aught° behold, of higher worth,   50
Than that inanimate cold world allowed
To the poor loveless ever-anxious crowd,
    Ah! from the soul itself must issue forth
A light, a glory, a fair luminous cloud
        Enveloping the Earth—   55
And from the soul itself must there be sent
    A sweet and potent voice, of its own birth,
Of all sweet sounds the life and element!

V

O pure of heart! thou need'st not ask of me
What this strong music in the soul may be!   60
    What, and wherein it doth exist,

°*Ours:* in our lives   °*aught:* anything

This light, this glory, this fair luminous mist,
This beautiful and beauty-making power,
    Joy, virtuous Lady! Joy that ne'er was given,
Save to the pure, and in their purest hour,   65
Life, and Life's effluence, cloud at once and shower,
Joy, Lady! is the spirit and the power,
Which wedding Nature to us gives in dower
    A new Earth and new Heaven,
Undreamt of by the sensual and the proud—   70
Joy is the sweet voice, Joy the luminous cloud—
    We in ourselves rejoice!
And thence flows all that charms or ear or sight,
    All melodies the echoes of that voice,
All colours a suffusion from that light.   75

VI

There was a time when, though my path was rough,
    This joy within me dallied with distress,
And all misfortunes were but as the stuff
    Whence Fancy made me dreams of happiness:
For hope grew round me, like the twining vine,   80
And fruits, and foliage, not my own, seemed mine.
But now afflictions bow me down to earth:
Nor care I that they rob me of my mirth;
    But oh! each visitation
Suspends what nature gave me at my birth,   85
    My shaping spirit of Imagination.
For not to think of what I needs must feel,
    But to be still and patient, all I can;
And haply by abstruse research to steal
    From my own nature all the natural man—   90
    This was my sole resource, my only plan:
Till that which suits a part infects the whole,
And now is almost grown the habit of my soul.

VII

Hence, viper thoughts, that coil around my mind,
    Reality's dark dream!   95
I turn from you, and listen to the wind,
    Which long has raved unnoticed. What a scream
Of agony by torture lengthened out
That lute sent forth! Thou Wind, that rav'st without,
    Bare crag, or mountain-tairn, or blasted tree,   100

Or pine-grove whither woodman never clomb,
Or lonely house, long held the witches' home,
   Methinks were fitter instruments for thee,   *Windham?*
Mad Lutanist! who in this month of showers,
Of dark-brown gardens, and of peeping flowers,   105
Mak'st Devils' yule, with worse than wintry song,
The blossoms, buds, and timorous leaves among.
   Thou Actor, perfect in all tragic sounds!
Thou mighty Poet, e'en to frenzy bold!
     What tell'st thou now about?   110
     'Tis of the rushing of an host in rout,
With groans, of trampled men, with smarting wounds—
At once they groan with pain, and shudder with the cold!
But hush! there is a pause of deepest silence!
    And all that noise, as of a rushing crowd,   115
With groans, and tremulous shudderings—all is over—
It tells another tale, with sounds less deep and loud!
    A tale of less affright,
    And tempered with delight,
As Otway's° self had framed the tender lay,—   120
    'Tis of a little child
    Upon a lonesome wild,
Not far from home, but she hath lost her way:
And now moans low in bitter grief and fear,
And now screams loud, and hopes to make her mother hear. 125

VIII

'Tis midnight, but small thoughts have I of sleep;
Full seldom may my friend such vigils keep!
Visit her, gentle Sleep! with wings of healing,
   And may this storm be but a mountain-birth,
May all the stars hang bright above her dwelling,   130
  Silent as though they watched the sleeping Earth!
    With light heart may she rise,
    Gay fancy, cheerful eyes,
  Joy lift her spirit, joy attune her voice;
To her may all things live, from pole to pole,   135
Their life the eddying of her living soul!
   O simple spirit, guided from above,
   Dear Lady! friend devoutest of my choice,
    Thus mayest thou ever, evermore rejoice.

°*Otway:*   Thomas Otway (1652–1685), author of *The Orphan*

Because Redemption is a psychological process, it is often dramatized by Romantic writers in symbolic form, with the changes and developments of the mind being set forth figuratively. "The Rime of the Ancient Mariner" is perhaps the best known and most accessible of these psychodramas. In it the psychological events are set forth in the figure of the voyage. Particular states of mind—self-consciousness, loss of spontaneity, separation from human connections, alienation and depression, and redemption to spiritual health—are illustrated through the events of the Mariner's experience, the weather, the sea, and the ship.

In outline, the passage of the Mariner from excessive confidence in Rationality, through a dark night of the soul, to Redemption, is represented by the Mariner's setting forth, full of confidence in the powers of analytic reason, confident that in leaving the safe and innocent church and town he is venturing to a future in which reason will elevate him. But the wind, which has been a servant, becomes a master of the ship, and the Mariner finds himself lost in the cold, icy latitudes where neither human nor animal life can exist. As a sign of salvation the Albatross comes, but the Mariner, with his spiritual sensitivity killed by reason, cannot participate in normal charity toward creatures, and he kills the bird for no reason. This act destroys his will, and he becomes becalmed, isolated, and alienated in ennui and despair, a man whose analytic habit has worn away all values, all meaning, all sympathetic identifications with others and all will to live. This state is one of living death. The natural world seems to him full of ghosts and horrid images, and his relationships with his fellows are guilt-ridden and destructive.

His Redemption occurs mysteriously, out of the inner forces possessed by the Self. The powers of Love(Joy) suddenly well up in him, and he is able without thought to bless the Water Snakes, to make gestures of love and affirmation toward the natural world, and perhaps toward the sexual forces it contains. This act of positive, creative will shows him that the forces of love and creativity are not dead. However, his Redemption takes a longer course, and although he can eventually return to his home country, he is a different man in a different state of mind, and his effect on those who have not experienced this passage is powerful and strange.

There is, of course, a great deal more to be said about the poem, and its power and fame are testimony to its richness, subtlety, and suggestiveness. Read closely and thoughtfully it provides a full acount of the inner psychological and spiritual forces and stages that the Romantic Redemption contains.

The poem begins with a Latin motto written in 1692 by the Anglican clergyman, Thomas Burnet. It emphasizes the belief that Reason and Science cannot know all that needs to be known:

I can easily believe that there are more invisible things in the universe than visible. But who can tell us their categories and ranks and relationships and particular features and activities? What do they do? Where do they live? The human mind has always reached toward these things, but has never touched them. I do not doubt, however, that it is sometimes worthwhile to consider in the mind, as if in a picture, the idea of a greater and better world; otherwise, the mind, too accustomed to small daily aspects of life may become too small, and subsist entirely on trivial thoughts. But, in the meantime, we must be vigilant for truth and observe proper proportions, that we may distinguish the certain from the uncertain, day from night.

THE RIME OF THE ANCIENT MARINER

Samuel Taylor Coleridge (1772–1836)

ARGUMENT

How a ship having passed the Line was driven by storms to the cold Country towards the South Pole; and how thence she made her course to the tropical Latitude of the Great Pacific Ocean; and of the strange things that befell; and in what manner the Ancient Mariner came back to his own Country.

I

An ancient Mariner meeteth three Gallants bidden to a wedding-feast, and detaineth one.

It is an ancient Mariner,
And he stoppeth one of three.
'By thy long grey beard and glittering eye,
Now wherefore stopp'st thou me?

The Bridegroom's doors are opened wide, 5
And I am next of kin;
The guests are met, the feast is set:
May'st hear the merry din.'

He holds him with his skinny hand,
'There was a ship,' quoth he. 10
'Hold off! unhand me, grey-beard loon!'
Eftsoons his hand dropt he.

The Wedding-Guest is spell-bound by the eye of the old seafaring man, and constrained to hear his tale.

He holds him with his glittering eye—
The Wedding-Guest stood still,
And listens like a three years' child: 15
The Mariner hath his will.

The Wedding-Guest sat on a stone:
He cannot choose but hear;
And thus spake on that ancient man,
The bright-eyed Mariner.   20

'The ship was cheered, the harbour cleared,
Merrily did we drop
Below the kirk, below the hill,
Below the lighthouse top.

The Mariner tells
how the ship
sailed southward
with a good wind
and fair weather,
till it reached the
line.
The Sun came up upon the left,   25
Out of the sea came he!
And he shone bright, and on the right
Went down into the sea.

Higher and higher every day,
Till over the mast at noon—'   30
The Wedding-Guest here beat his breast,
For he heard the loud bassoon.

The Wedding-
Guest heareth the
bridal music; but
the Mariner con-
tinueth his tale.
The bride hath paced into the hall,
Red as a rose is she;
Nodding their heads before her goes   35
The merry minstrelsy.

The Wedding-Guest he beat his breast,
Yet he cannot choose but hear;
And thus spake on that ancient man,
The bright-eyed Mariner.   40

The ship drawn
by a storm toward
the south pole.
'And now the STORM-BLAST came, and he
Was tyrannous and strong:
He struck with his o'ertaking wings,
And chased us south along.

The land of ice,
and of fearful
sounds where no
living thing was
to be seen.
With sloping masts and dipping prow,   45
As who pursued with yell and blow
Still treads the shadow of his foe,
And forward bends his head,
The ship drove fast, loud roared the blast,
And southward aye we fled.   50

And now there came both mist and snow,
And it grew wondrous cold:

And ice, mast-high, came floating by,
As green as emerald.

And through the drifts the snowy clifts   55
Did send a dismal sheen:
Nor shapes of men nor beasts we ken—
The ice was all between.

The ice was here, the ice was there,
The ice was all around: 60
It cracked and growled, and roared and howled,
Like noises in a swound!°

Till a great sea-
bird, called the
Albatross, came
through the snow-
fog, and was re-
ceived with great
joy and hospital-
ity.
At length did cross an Albatross,
Thorough the fog it came;
As if it had been a Christian soul,   65
We hailed it in God's name.

It ate the food it ne'er had eat,
and round and round it flew,
The ice did split with a thunder-fit;
The helmsman steered us through!   70

And lo! the Alba-
tross proveth a
bird of good
omen, and follow-
eth the ship as it
returned north-
ward through fog
and floating ice.
And a good south wind sprung up behind;
The Albatross did follow,
And every day, for food or play,
Came to the mariners' hollo!

In mist or cloud, on mast or shroud,   75
It perched for vespers nine;
Whiles all the night, through fog-smoke white,
Glimmered the white Moon-shine.'

The ancient Mari-
ner inhospitably
killeth the pious
bird of good
omen.
'God save thee, ancient Mariner!
From the fiends, that plague thee thus!—   80
Why look'st thou so?'—'With my cross-bow
I shot the ALBATROSS.'

II

'The Sun now rose upon the right:
Out of the sea came he,

°*swound:* swoon

Still hid in mist, and on the left   85
Went down into the sea.

And the good south wind still blew behind,
But no sweet bird did follow,
Nor any day for food or play
Came to the mariners' hollo!   90

His shipmates cry out against the ancient Mariner for killing the bird of good luck.

And I had done a hellish thing,
And it would work 'em woe:
For all averred, I had killed the bird
That made the breeze to blow.
Ah wretch! said they, the bird to slay,   95
That made the breeze to blow!

But when the fog cleared off, they justify the same, and thus make themselves accomplices in the crime.

Nor dim nor red, like God's own head,
The glorious Sun uprist:
Then all averred, I had killed the bird
That brought the fog and mist.   100
'Twas right, said they, such birds to slay,
That bring the fog and mist.

The fair breeze continues; the ship enters the Pacific Ocean, and sails northward, even till it reaches the line.

The fair breeze blew, the white foam flew,
The furrow followed free;
We were the first that ever burst   105
Into that silent sea.

Down dropt the breeze, the sails dropt down,
'Twas sad as sad could be;
And we did speak only to break
The silence of the sea!   110

The ship hath been suddenly becalmed.

All in a hot and copper sky,
The bloody Sun, at noon,
Right up above the mast did stand,
No bigger than the Moon.

Day after day, day after day,   115
We stuck, nor breath nor motion;
As idle as a painted ship
Upon a painted ocean.

Water, water, every where,
And all the boards did shrink;   120
Water, water, every where,
Nor any drop to drink.

The very deep did rot: O Christ!
That ever this should be!
Yea, slimy things did crawl with legs   125
Upon the slimy sea.

About, about, in reel and rout
The death-fires danced at night;
The water, like a witch's oils,
Burnt green, and blue and white.   130

And some in dreams assuréd were
Of the Spirit that plagued us so;
Nine fathom deep he had followed us
From the land of mist and snow.

A Spirit had fol-
lowed them; one
of the invisible in-
habitants of this
planet, neither de-
parted souls nor
angels; concern-
ing whom the
learned Jew, Jo-
sephus, and the
Platonic Constan-
tinopolitan, Mi-
chael Psellus, may
be consulted.
They are very nu-
merous, and there
is no climate or

And every tongue, through utter drought,   135
Was withered at the root;
We could not speak, no more than if
We had been choked with soot.

Ah! well a-day! what evil looks
Had I from old and young!   140
Instead of the cross, the Albatross
About my neck was hung.'

element without one or more. The shipmates, in their sore distress, would fain
throw the whole guilt on the ancient Mariner: in sign whereof they hang the
dead seabird round his neck.

III

The ancient Mari-
ner beholdeth a
sign in the ele-
ment afar off.

'There passed a weary time. Each throat
Was parched, and glazed each eye.
A weary time! a weary time!   145
How glazed each weary eye,
When looking westward, I beheld
A something in the sky.

At first it seemed a little speck,
And then it seemed a mist;   150

It moved and moved, and took at last
A certain shape, I wist.°

A speck, a mist, a shape, I wist!
And still it neared and neared:
As if it dodged a water-sprite,   155
It plunged and tacked and veered.

At its nearer approach, it seemeth him to be a ship; and at a dear ransom he freeth his speech from the bonds of thirst. A flash of joy;

With throats unslaked, with black lips baked,
We could nor laugh nor wail;
Through utter drought all dumb we stood!
I bit my arm, I sucked the blood,   160
And cried, "A sail! a sail!"

With throats unslaked, with black lips baked,
Agape they heard me call:
Gramercy! they for joy did grin,
And all at once their breath drew in,   165
As they were drinking all.

And horror follows. For can it be a ship that comes onward without wind or tide?

"See! see!" (I cried) "she tacks no more!
Hither to work us weal;°
Without a breeze, without a tide,
She steadies with upright keel!"   170

The western wave was all a-flame.
The day was well nigh done!
Almost upon the western wave
Rested the broad bright Sun;
When that strange shape drove suddenly   175
Betwixt us and the Sun.

It seemeth him but the skeleton of a ship.

And straight the Sun was flecked with bars,
(Heaven's Mother send us grace!)
As if through a dungeon-grate he peered
With broad and burning face.   180

Alas! (thought I, and my heart beat loud)
How fast she nears and nears!
Are those *her* sails that glance in the Sun,
Like restless gossameres?

°*wist:* knew   °*weal:* good

And its ribs are seen as bars on the face of the setting sun.	Are those *her* ribs through which the Sun 185 Did peer, as through a grate? And is that Woman all her crew? Is that a DEATH? and are there two? Is DEATH that woman's mate?
The Spectre-Woman and her Death-mate, and no other on board the skeleton-ship. Like vessel, like crew!	*Her* lips were red, *her* looks were free, 190 Her locks were yellow as gold: Her skin was as white as leprosy, The Night-mare LIFE-IN-DEATH was she, Who thicks man's blood with cold.
Death and Life-in-Death have diced for the ship's crew, and she (the latter) winneth the ancient Mariner.	The naked hulk alongside came, 195 And the twain were casting dice; "The game is done! I've won! I've won!" Quoth she, and whistles thrice.
	The Sun's rim dips; the stars rush out: At one stride comes the dark; 200 With far-heard whisper, o'er the sea, Off shot the spectre-bark.
	We listened and looked sideways up! Fear at my heart, as at a cup, My life-blood seemed to sip! 205
No twilight within the courts of the sun.	The stars were dim, and thick the night, The steersman's face by his lamp gleamed white; From the sails the dew did drip—
At the rising of the moon	Till clomb above the eastern bar The hornéd Moon, with one bright star 210 Within the nether tip.°
One after another, His shipmates drop down dead.	One after one, by the star-dogged Moon, Too quick for groan or sigh, Each turned his face with a ghastly pang, And cursed me with his eye. 215
	Four times fifty living men, (And I heard nor sigh nor groan) With heavy thump, a lifeless lump, They dropped down one by one.

°*Moon . . . tip:* "It is a common superstition among sailors that something evil is about to happen whenever a star dogs the moon" [Coleridge's note].

But Life-in-Death
begins her work
on the ancient
Mariner.

The souls did from their bodies fly,—
They fled to bliss or woe!
And every soul, it passed me by,
Like the whizz of my cross-bow!'

IV

The Wedding-
Guest feareth that
a spirit is talking
to him;

'I fear thee, ancient Mariner!
I fear thy skinny hand!
And thou art long, and lank, and brown,
As is the ribbed sea-sand.

I fear thee and thy glittering eye,
And thy skinny hand, so brown.'—
'Fear not, fear not, thou Wedding-Guest!
This body dropt not down.

But the ancient
Mariner assureth
him of his bodily
life, and proceed-
eth to relate his
horrible penance.

Alone, alone, all, all alone,
Alone on a wide wide sea!
And never a saint took pity on
My soul in agony.

He despiseth the
creatures of the
calm,

The many men, so beautiful!
And they all dead did lie:
And a thousand thousand slimy things
Lived on; and so did I.

And envieth that
they should live,
and so many be
dead.

I looked upon the rotting sea,
And drew my eyes away;
I looked upon the rotting deck,
And there the dead men lay.

I looked to heaven, and tried to pray;
But or ever a prayer had gusht,
A wicked whisper came, and made
My heart as dry as dust.

I closed my lids, and kept them close,
And the balls like pulses beat;
For the sky and the sea, and the sea and the sky
Lay like a load on my weary eye,
And the dead were at my feet.

225

230

235

240

245

250

But the curse liv-
eth for him in the
eye of the dead
men.

The cold sweat melted from their limbs,
Nor rot nor reek did they:
The look with which they looked on me   255
Had never passed away.

An orphan's curse would drag to hell
A spirit from on high;
But oh! more horrible than that
Is the curse in a dead man's eye!   260
Seven days, seven nights, I saw that curse,
And yet I could not die.

The moving Moon went up the sky,
And no where did abide:

In his loneliness
and fixedness he
yearneth towards
the journeying
moon, and the
stars that still so-
journ, yet still
move onward;
and every where
the blue sky be-
longs to them,
and is their ap-
pointed rest, and their native country and their own natural homes, which they
enter unannounced, as lords that are certainly expected and yet there is a silent
joy at their arrival.
By the light of the
moon he behold-
eth God's crea-
tures of the great
calm.

Softly she was going up,
And a star or two beside—   265

Her beams bemocked the sultry main,
Like April hoar-frost spread;
But where the ship's huge shadow lay,
The charméd water burnt alway
A still and awful red.   270

Beyond the shadow of the ship,
I watched the water-snakes:
They moved in tracks of shining white,
And when they reared, the elfish light   275
Fell off in hoary flakes.

Within the shadow of the ship
I watched their rich attire:
Blue, glossy green, and velvet black,
They coiled and swam; and every track   280
Was a flash of golden fire.

O happy living things! no tongue
Their beauty might declare:
A spring of love gushed from my heart,

And I blessed them unaware: 285
Sure my kind saint took pity on me,
And I blessed them unaware.

The self-same moment I could pray;
And from my neck so free
The Albatross fell off, and sank   290
Like lead into the sea.'

V

'Oh sleep! it is a gentle thing.
Beloved from pole to pole!
To Mary Queen the praise be given!
She sent the gentle sleep from Heaven,   295
That slid into my soul.

By grace of the
holy Mother, the
ancient Mariner is
refreshed with
rain.

The silly buckets on the deck,
That had so long remained,
I dreamt that they were filled with dew;
And when I awoke, it rained.   300

My lips were wet, my throat was cold,
My garments all were dank;
Sure I had drunken in my dreams,
And still my body drank.

I moved, and could not feel my limbs: 305
I was so light—almost
I thought that I had died in sleep,
And was a blessèd ghost.

He heareth sounds
and seeth strange
sights and com-
motions in the
sky and the ele-
ment.

And soon I heard a roaring wind:
It did not come anear;   310
But with its sound it shook the sails,
That were so thin and sere.

The upper air burst into life!
And a hundred fire-flags sheen,
To and fro they were hurried about!   315
And to and fro, and in and out,
The wan stars danced between.

And the coming wind did roar more loud,
And the sails did sigh like sedge;
And the rain poured down from one black cloud;   320
The Moon was at its edge.

The thick black cloud was cleft, and still
The Moon was at its side:
Like waters shot from some high crag,
The lightning fell with never a jag,   325
A river steep and wide.

The bodies of the ship's crew are inspired, and the ship moves on.
The loud wind never reached the ship,
Yet now the ship moved on!
Beneath the lightning and the Moon
The dead men gave a groan.   330

They groaned, they stirred, they all uprose,
Nor spake, nor moved their eyes;
It had been strange, even in a dream,
To have seen those dead men rise.

The helmsman steered, the ship moved on;   335
Yet never a breeze up-blew;
The mariners all 'gan work the ropes,
Where they were wont to do;
They raised their limbs like lifeless tools—
We were a ghastly crew.   340

The body of my brother's son
Stood by me, knee to knee:
The body and I pulled at one rope,
But he said nought to me.'

'I fear thee, ancient Mariner!'   345
'Be calm, thou Wedding-Guest!
But not by the souls of the men, nor by demons of earth or middle air, but by a blessed troop of angelic spirits, sent down by the invocation of the guardian saint.
'Twas not those souls that fled in pain,
Which to their corses came again,
But a troop of spirits blest:

For when it dawned—they dropped their arms,   350
And clustered round the mast;
Sweet sounds rose slowly through their mouths,
And from their bodies passed.

Around, around, flew each sweet sound,
Then darted to the Sun;   355
Slowly the sounds came back again,
Now mixed, now one by one.

Sometimes a-dropping from the sky
I heard the sky-lark sing;
Sometimes all little birds that are,   360
How they seemed to fill the sea and air
With their sweet jargoning!

And now 'twas like all instruments,
Now like a lonely flute;
And now it is an angel's song,   365
That makes the heavens be mute.

It ceased; yet still the sails made on
A pleasant noise till noon,
A noise like of a hidden brook
In the leafy month of June,   370
That to the sleeping woods all night
Singeth a quiet tune.

Till noon we quietly sailed on,
Yet never a breeze did breathe:
Slowly and smoothly went the ship,   375
Moved onward from beneath.

The lonesome
Spirit from the
south pole carries
on the ship as far
as the line, in
obedience to the
angelic troop, but
still requireth
vengeance.

Under the keel nine fathom deep,
From the land of mist and snow,
The spirit slid: and it was he
That made the ship to go.   380
The sails at noon left off their tune,
And the ship stood still also.

The Sun, right up above the mast,
Had fixed her to the ocean:
But in a minute she 'gan stir,   385
With a short uneasy motion—
Backwards and forwards half her length
With a short uneasy motion.

Then like a pawing horse let go,
She made a sudden bound: 390
It flung the blood into my head,
And I fell down in a swound.

How long in that same fit I lay,
I have not to declare;

But ere my living life returned,   395
I heard and in my soul discerned
Two voices in the air.

"Is it he?" quoth one, "Is this the man?
By him who died on cross,
With his cruel bow he laid full low   400
The harmless Albatross.

The spirit who bideth by himself
In the land of mist and snow,
He loved the bird that loved the man
Who shot him with his bow."   405

The other was a softer voice,
As soft as honey-dew:
Quoth he, "The man hath penance done,
And penance more will do." '

VI

First Voice

' "But tell me, tell me! speak again,   410
Thy soft response renewing—
What makes that ship drive on so fast?
What is the ocean doing?"

Second Voice

"Still as a slave before his lord,
The ocean hath no blast;   415
His great bright eye most silently
Up to the Moon is cast—

If he may know which way to go;
For she guides him smooth or grim.
See, brother, see! how graciously
She looketh down on him."   420

First Voice

The Mariner hath been cast into a trance; for the angelic power causeth the vessel to drive northward faster than human life could endure.

"But why drives on that ship so fast,
Without or wave or wind?"

"The air is cut away before,
And closes from behind.   425

Fly, brother, fly! more high, more high!
Or we shall be belated:
For slow and slow that ship will go,
When the Mariner's trance is abated."

The supernatural motion is retarded; the Mariner awakes and his penance begins anew.	I woke, and we were sailing on 430

I woke, and we were sailing on   430
As in a gentle weather:
'Twas night, calm night, the moon was high;
The dead men stood together.

All stood together on the deck,
For a charnel-dungeon fitter: 435
All fixed on me their stony eyes,
That in the Moon did glitter.

The pang, the curse, with which they died,
Had never passed away:
I could not draw my eyes from theirs,   440
Nor turn them up to pray.

The curse is finally expiated.

And now this spell was snapt: once more
I viewed the ocean green,
And looked far forth, yet little saw
Of what had else been seen—   445

Like one, that on a lonesome road
Doth walk in fear and dread,
And having once turned round walks on,
And turns no more his head;
Because he knows, a frightful fiend   450
Doth close behind him tread.

But soon there breathed a wind on me,
Nor sound nor motion made:
Its path was not upon the sea,
In ripple or in shade.   455

It raised my hair, it fanned my cheek
Like a meadow-gale of spring—

It mingled strangely with my fears,
Yet it felt like a welcoming.

Swiftly, swiftly flew the ship,   460
Yet she sailed softly too:
Sweetly, sweetly blew the breeze—
On me alone it blew.

Oh! dream of joy! is this indeed
The light-house top I see?   465
Is this the hill? is this the kirk?
Is this mine own countree?

We drifted o'er the harbour-bar,
And I with sobs did pray—
O let me be awake, my God!   470
Or let me sleep alway.

The harbour-bay was clear as glass,
So smoothly it was strewn!
And on the bay the moonlight lay,
And the shadow of the Moon.   475

The rock shone bright, the kirk no less,
That stands above the rock:
The moonlight steeped in silentness
The steady weathercock.

And the bay was white with silent light,   480
Till rising from the same,
Full many shapes, that shadows were,
In crimson colours came.

A little distance from the prow
Those crimson shadows were: 485
I turned my eyes upon the deck—
Oh, Christ! what saw I there!

Each corse lay flat, lifeless and flat,
And, by the holy rood!°
A man all light, a seraph-man,   490
On every corse there stood.

°*rood:* cross

This seraph-band, each waved his hand:
It was a heavenly sight!
They stood as signals to the land,
Each one a lovely light;   495

This seraph-band, each waved his hand,
No voice did they impart—
No voice; but oh! the silence sank
Like music on my heart.

But soon I heard the dash of oars,   500
I heard the Pilot's cheer;
My head was turned perforce away
And I saw a boat appear.

The Pilot and the Pilot's boy,
I heard them coming fast: 505
Dear Lord in Heaven! it was a joy
The dead men could not blast.

I saw a third—I heard his voice:
It is the Hermit good!
He singeth loud his godly hymns   510
That he makes in the wood.
He'll shrieve my soul, he'll wash away
The Albatross's blood.'

VII

The Hermit of the wood,

'This Hermit good lives in that wood
Which slopes down to the sea.   515
How loudly his sweet voice he rears!
He loves to talk with marineres
That come from a far countree.

He kneels at morn, and noon, and eve—
He hath a cushion plump: 520
It is the moss that wholly hides
The rotted old oak-stump.

The skiff-boat neared: I heard them talk,
"Why, this is strange, I trow!
Where are those lights so many and fair,   525
That signal made but now?"

Approacheth the
ship with wonder.
"Strange, by my faith!" the Hermit said—
"And they answered not our cheer!
The planks looked warped! and see those sails,
How thin they are and sere!   530
I never saw aught like to them,
Unless perchance it were

Brown skeletons of leaves that lag
My forest-brook along;
When the ivy-tod is heavy with snow,   535
And the owlet whoops to the wolf below,
That eats the she-wolf's young."

"Dear Lord! it hath a fiendish look—
(The Pilot made reply)
"I am a-feared"—"Push on, push on!"   540
Said the Hermit cheerily.

The boat came closer to the ship,
But I nor spake nor stirred;
The boat came close beneath the ship,
And straight a sound was heard.   545

The ship suddenly
sinketh.
Under the water it rumbled on,
Still louder and more dread:
It reached the ship, it split the bay;
The ship went down like lead.

Stunned by that loud and dreadful sound,   550
Which sky and ocean smote,
Like one that hath been seven days drowned
My body lay afloat;
The ancient Mari-
ner is saved in the
pilot's boat.
But swift as dreams, myself I found
Within the Pilot's boat.   555

Upon the whirl, where sank the ship,
The boat spun round and round;
And all was still, save that the hill
Was telling of the sound.

I moved my lips—the Pilot shrieked   560
And fell down in a fit;
The holy hermit raised his eyes,
And prayed where he did sit.

I took the oars: the Pilot's boy,
Who now doth crazy go,   565
Laughed loud and long, and all the while
His eyes went to and fro.
"Ha! ha!" quoth he, "full plain I see,
The Devil knows how to row."

And now, all in my own countree,   570
I stood on the firm land!
The Hermit stepped forth from the boat,
And scarcely he could stand.

The ancient Mariner earnestly entreateth the Hermit to shrieve him; and the penance of life falls on him.

"O shrieve me, shrieve me, holy man!"
The Hermit crossed his brow.   575
"Say quick," quoth he, "I bid thee say—
What manner of man art thou?"

Forthwith this frame of mine was wrenched
With a woful agony,
Which forced me to begin my tale;   580
And then it left me free.

And ever and anon throughout his future life an agony constraineth him to travel from land to land,

Since then, at an uncertain hour,
That agony returns:
And till my ghastly tale is told,
This heart within me burns.   585

I pass, like night, from land to land;
I have strange power of speech;
That moment that his face I see,
I know the man that must hear me:
To him my tale I teach.   590

What loud uproar bursts from that door!
The wedding-guests are there:
But in the garden-bower the bride
And bride-maids singing are:
And hark the little vesper bell,   595
Which biddeth me to prayer!

O Wedding-Guest! this soul hath been
Alone on a wide wide sea:
So lonely 'twas, that God himself
Scarce seeméd there to be.   600

O sweeter than the marriage-feast,
'Tis sweeter far to me,
To walk together to the kirk
With a goodly company!—

To walk together to the kirk, 605
And all together pray,
While each to his great Father bends,
Old men, and babes, and loving friends
And youths and maidens gay!

Farewell, farewell! but this I tell 610
To thee, thou Wedding-Guest!
And to teach, by his own example, love and reverence to all things that God made and loveth. He prayeth well, who loveth well
Both man and bird and beast.

He prayeth best, who loveth best
All things both great and small; 615
For the dear God who loveth us,
He made and loveth all.'

The Mariner, whose eye is bright,
Whose beard with age is hoar,
Is gone: and now the Wedding-Guest 620
Turned from the bridegroom's door.

He went like one that hath been stunned,
And is of sense forlorn:
A sadder and a wiser man,
He rose the morrow morn. 625

*   *   *

The following essay summarizes the dangers of this "disease" of self-consciousness and the ways in which Romantic poems overcame this condition. Bloom's citation of examples suggests the variety of works and writers who worked through this problem and the variety of strategies used for this purpose.

ROMANTICISM AND ANTI-SELF-CONSCIOUSNESS

Geoffrey Hartman (1929-   )

The dejection afflicting John Stuart Mill in his twentieth year was alleviated by two important events. He read Wordsworth, and he discovered for himself a view of life resembling the "anti-self-consciousness theory" of Carlyle. Mill describes this strangely named theory in his *Autobiography:*

> Ask yourself whether you are happy, and you cease to be so. The only chance is to treat, not happiness, but some end external to it as the purpose of life. Let your self-consciousness, your scrutiny, your self-interrogation exhaust themselves on that.

It is not surprising that Wordsworth's poetry should also have served to protect Mill from the morbidity of his intellect. Like many Romantics, Wordsworth had passed through a depression clearly linked to the ravage of self-consciousness and the "strong disease" of self-analysis. Book 11 of *The Prelude,*° chapter 5 of Mill's *Autobiography,* Carlyle's *Sartor Resartus,* and other great confessional works of the Romantic period show how crucial these maladies are for the adolescent mind. Endemic, perhaps, to every stage of life, they especially affect the transition from adolescence to maturity; and it is interesting to observe how man's attention has shifted from the fact of death and its rites of passage, to these trials in what Keats called "the Chamber of Maiden-Thought" and, more recently still, to the perils of childhood. We can say, taking a metaphor from Donne, that "streights, and none but streights" are ways to whatever changes the mind must undergo, and that it is the Romantics who first explored the dangerous passageways of maturation.

Two trials or perils of the soul deserve special mention. We learn that every increase in consciousness is accompanied by an increase in self-consciousness, and that analysis can easily become a passion that "murders to dissect." These difficulties of thought in its strength question the ideal of absolute lucidity. The issue is raised of whether there exist what might be called *remedia intellectus:* remedies for the corrosive power of analysis and the fixated self-consciousness.

There is one remedy of great importance which is almost coterminous with art itself in the Romantic period. This remedy differs from certain traditional proposals linked to the religious control of the intellect—the wild, living intellect of man, as Newman calls it in his

---

Reprinted from *The Centennial Review* by permission of the author and the publisher.

°The *Prelude:*   Wordsworth's long, autobiographical poem; it too tells of despair and redemption.

Apologia. A particularly Romantic remedy, it is nonlimiting with respect to the mind. It seeks to draw the antidote to self-consciousness from consciousness itself. A way is to be found not to escape from or limit knowledge, but to convert it into an energy finer than intellectual. It is some such thought which makes Wordsworth in the preface to *Lyrical Ballads* describe poetry as the "breath and finer spirit of all knowledge," able to carry sensation into the midst of the most abstract or remotest objects of science. A more absolute figure for this cure, which is, strictly speaking, less a cure than a paradoxical faith, is given by Kleist: "Paradise is locked . . . yet to return to the state of innocence we must eat once more of the tree of knowledge." It is not by accident that Kleist is quoted by Adrian at a significant point in Mann's *Doktor Faustus*, which is *the* novel about self-consciousness and its relation to art. . . .

The link between consciousness and self-consciousness, or knowledge and guilt, is already expressed in the story of the expulsion from Eden. Having tasted knowledge, man realizes his nakedness, his sheer separateness of self. I have quoted Kleist's reflection; and Hegel, in his interpretation of the Fall, argues that the way back to Eden is via contraries: the naively sensuous mind must pass through separation and selfhood to become spiritually perfect. It is the destiny of consciousness or, as the English Romantics would have said, of imagination, to separate from nature so that it can finally transcend not only nature but also its own lesser forms. Hegel in his *Logic* puts it as follows:

> The first reflection of awakened consciousness in men told them they were naked. . . . The hour that man leaves the path of mere natural being marks the difference between him, a self-conscious agent, and the natural world. The spiritual is distinguished from the natural . . . in that it does not continue a mere stream of tendency, but sunders itself to self-realization. But this position of severed life has in its turn to be overcome, and the spirit must, by its own act, achieve concord once more. . . . The principle of restoration is found in thought, and thought only: the hand that inflicts the wound is also the hand that heals it.

The last sentence states unequivocally where the remedy lies. Hegel, however, does not honor the fact that the meaning he derives from the Fall was originally in the form of myth. And the attempt to think mythically° is itself part of a crucial defense against the self-conscious intellect. Bergson in *The Two Sources of Morality and Religion* sees both myth and religion as products of an intellectual instinct created by nature itself to

---

°*to think mythically:* i.e., to embody ideas and values in a fictional, symbolic context, giving them an emotional reality. For fuller discussion of this idea see the volume in this series, *Symbol and Myth in Modern Literature.*

oppose the analytic intellect, to preserve human spontaneities despite the hesitant and complicated mind. Whether myth-making is still possible, whether the mind can find an unselfconscious medium for itself or maintain something of the interacting unity of self and life, is a central concern of the Romantic poets.

Romantic art as myth-making has been discussed convincingly in recent years, and Friedrich Schlegel's call in "Rede über die Mythologie" (1800) for a modern mythology is well known. The question of the renewal of myth is, nevertheless, a rather special response to the larger perplexities of reflective thought. "The poet," says Wallace Stevens in "Adagia," "represents the mind in the act of defending us against itself." Starting with the Romantics, this act is clearly focused, and poetry begins to be valued in contradistinction to directly analytic or purely conceptual modes of thought. The intelligence is seen as a perverse though necessary specialization of the whole soul of man, and art as a means to resist the intelligence intelligently.

It must be admitted, at the same time, that the Romantics themselves do not give (in their conceptual moments) an adequate definition of the function of art. Their criterion of pleasure or expressive emotion leads to some kind of art for art's sake formula, or to the sentimentalism which Mill still shared and which marks the shift in sensibility from Neoclassic to Romantic. That Mill wept over the memoirs of Marmontel and felt his selfhood lightened by this evidence of his ability to feel, or that Lamartine saw the life of the poet as "tears and love," suggests that the *larmoyant°* vein of the later eighteenth century persisted for some time but also helped, when tears or even joy were translated into theory, to falsify the Romantic achievement and make Irving Babbitt's° criticism possible.

The art of the Romantics, on the other hand, is often in advance of even their best thoughts. Neither a mere increase in sensibility nor a mere widening of self-knowledge constitutes its purpose. The Romantic poets do not exalt consciousness per se. They have recognized it as a kind of death-in-life, as the product of a division in the self. The mind which acknowledges the existence or past existence of immediate life knows that its present strength is based on a separation from that life. A creative mind desires not mere increase of knowledge, but "knowledge not purchased by the loss of power" (*The Prelude, 5*). Life, says Ruskin, is the only wealth; yet childhood, or certain irrevocable moments, confront the poet sharply and give him the sense of having purchased with death the life of the mind. Constructing what Yeats calls an anti-self, or recovering deeply buried experience, the poet seeks a return to "Unity of Being." Consciousness is only a middle term, the strait through which everything must

---

°*larmoyant:* weepy   °*Babbitt:* Irving Babbitt (1865–1933), who, in *Rousseau and Romanticism*, attacks romantic thought for being feeble, utopian, and uncritically dreamy

pass; and the artist plots to have everything pass through whole, without sacrifice to abstraction.

One of the themes which best expresses this perilous nature of consciousness and which has haunted literature since the Romantic period is that of the Solitary, or Wandering Jew. He may appear as Cain, Ahasuerus, Ancient Mariner, and even Faust. He also resembles the later (and more static) figures of Tithonus,° Gerontion,° and *poète maudit.*° These solitaries are separated from life in the midst of life, yet cannot die. They are doomed to live a middle or purgatorial existence which is neither life nor death, and as their knowledge increases so does their solitude. It is, ultimately, consciousness that alienates them from life and imposes the burden of a self which religion or death or a return to the state of nature might dissolve. Yet their heroism, or else their doom, is not to obtain this release. Rebels against God, like Cain, and men of God, like Vigny's Moses, are equally denied "le sommeil de la terre" and are shown to suffer the same despair, namely, "the self . . . whose worm dieth not, and whose fire is not quenched" (Kierkegaard). And in Coleridge's Mariner, as in Conrad's Marlow, the figure of the wanderer approaches that of the poet. Both are storytellers who resubmit themselves to temporality and are compelled to repeat their experiences in the purgatorial form of words. Yeats, deeply affected by the theme of the Wandering Jew, records a marvelous comment of Mme. Blavatsky's: "I write, write, write, as the Wandering Jew walks, walks, walks."

The Solitary may also be said to create his own, peculiarly Romantic genre of poetry. In "Tintern Abbey," or "X" Revisited,° the poet looks back at a transcended stage and comes to grips with the fact of self-alienation. The retrospective movement may be visionary, as often in Hölderlin; or antiquarian, as in Scott; or deeply oblique, as in lyrical ballad and monologue. In every case, however, there is some confrontation of person with shadow or self with self. The intense lyricism of the Romantics may well be related to this confrontation. For the Romantic "I" emerges nostalgically when certainty and simplicity of self are lost. In a lyric poem it is clearly not the first-person form that moves us (the poem need not be in the first person) but rather the I toward which that I reaches. The very confusion in modern literary theory concerning the fictive I, whether it represents the writer as person or only as persona, may reflect a dialectic inherent in poetry between the relatively self-conscious self and that self within the self which resembles Blake's "emanation" and Shelley's "epipsyche."

°*Tithonus and Gerontion:* alienated personae from poems by Tennyson and Eliot   °*poète maudit:* the accursed or "sick" poet   °*"X" Revisited:* the strategy of such poems is to compare an innocent unself-conscious "then" with a fallen hyperconscious "now"

It is true, of course, that this dialectic is found in every age and not restricted to the Romantic. The notion of man (as of history) seems to presuppose that of self-consciousness, and art is not the only major reaction to it. Mircea Eliade, following Nietzsche, has recently linked art to religion by interpreting the latter as originating in a periodic and ritually controlled abolition of the burden of self, or rather of this burden in the form of a nascent historical sense. It is not true, according to Eliade, that primitive man has no sense of history; on the contrary, his sense of it is too acute, he cannot tolerate the weight of responsibility accruing through memory and individuation, and only gradually does religious myth, and especially the Judaeo-Christian revelation, teach him to become a more conscious historical being. The question, therefore, is why the Romantic reaction to the problem of self-consciousness should be in the form of an aggrandizement of art, and why the entire issue should now achieve an urgency and explicitness previously lacking.

The answer requires a distinction between religion and art. This distinction can take a purely historical form. There clearly comes a time when art frees itself from its subordination to religion or religiously inspired myth and continues or even replaces them. This time seems to coincide with what is generally called the Romantic period: the latter, at least, is a good *terminus a quo.*° Though every age may find its own means to convert self-consciousness into the larger energy of imagination, in the Romantic period it is primarily art on which this crucial function devolves. Thus, for Blake, all religion is a derivation of the Poetic Genius; and Matthew Arnold is already matter-of-fact rather than prophetic about a new age in which the religious passion is preserved chiefly by poetry. If Romantic poetry appears to the orthodox as misplaced religious feeling ("spilt religion"),° to the Romantics themselves it redeems religion.

Yet as soon as poetry is separated from imposed religious or communal ends it becomes as problematic as the individual himself. The question of how art is possible, though post-Romantic in its explicitness, has its origin here, for the artist is caught up in a serious paradox. His art is linked to the autonomous and individual; yet that same art, in the absence of an authoritative myth, must bear the entire weight of having to transcend or ritually limit these tendencies. No wonder the problem of the subjective, the isolated, the individual, grows particularly acute. Subjectivity—even solipsism°—becomes the subject of poems which qua poetry seek to transmute it.

°*terminus a quo:* beginning point   °*spilt religion:* an accusation made by T.E. Hulme. The concept summarizes the view of those whose religious myths and beliefs remain Christian. For them, Romantic efforts to regain innocence and purity of Self are unnecessary, since the Self is purified by God's Grace.
°*solipsism:* creating an external reality out of one's inner subjectivity, and becoming deluded about its origin; or more simply, attributing too much truth to one's inner state. Since each poet must make his own mythology, the act of attempting this can push the poet into more extreme states of self-consciousness. See Part VI.

This paradox seems to inhere in all the seminal works of the Romantic period. "Thus my days are passed / In contradiction," Wordsworth writes sadly at the beginning of *The Prelude*. He cannot decide whether he is fit to be a poet on an epic scale. The great longing is there; the great (objective) theme eludes him. Wordsworth cannot find his theme because he already has it: himself. Yet he knows self-consciousness to be at once necessary and opposed to poetry. It will take him the whole of *The Prelude* to be satisfied *in actu* that he is a poet. His poem, beginning in the vortex of self-consciousness, is carried to epic length in the desire to prove that his former imaginative powers are not dead.

I have already confessed to understanding the *Ancient Mariner* as a poem that depicts the soul after its birth to the sense of separate (and segregated) being. In one of the really magical poems in the language, which, generically, converts self-consciousness into imagination. Coleridge describes the travail of a soul passing from self-consciousness to imagination. The slaying of an innocent creature, the horror of statis, the weight of conscience or of the vertical eye (the sun), the appearance of the theme of deathlessness, and the terrible repetitive process of penitence whereby the wanderer becomes aware through the spirits above and the creatures below of his focal solitude between both—these point with archetypal force to the burden of selfhood, the straits of solitude, and the compensating plenary imagination that grows inwardly. The poem opens by evoking that *rite de passage* we call a wedding and which leads to full human communion, but the Mariner's story interposes itself as a reminder of human separateness and of the intellectual love (in Spinoza's sense) made possible by it.

To explore the transition from self-consciousness to imagination and to achieve that transition while exploring it (and so to prove it still possible) is the Romantic purpose I find most crucial. The precariousness of that transition naturally evokes the idea of a journey; and in some later poets, like Rimbaud and Hart Crane, the motif of the journey has actually become a sustained metaphor for the experience of the artist during creation. This journey, of course, does not lead to what is generally called a truth: some final station for the mind. It remains as problematic a crossing as that from death to second life or from exile to redemption. These religious concepts, moreover, are often blended in and remind us that Romantic art has a function analogous to that of religion. The traditional scheme of Eden, Fall, and Redemption merges with the new triad of Nature, Self-Consciousness, and Imagination—the last term in both involving a kind of return to the first.

Yet everything depends on whether it is the right and fruitful return. For the journey beyond self-consciousness is shadowed by cyclicity, by paralysis before the endlessness of introspection, and by the lure of false ultimates. Blake's "Mental Traveller," Browning's "Childe Roland to The Dark Tower Came," and Emily Dickinson's "Our journey had advanced" show these dangers in some of their forms. Nature in its childhood or sensuous radiance (Blake's "Beulah") exerts an especially deceptive lure. The desire to gain truth, finality, or revelation generates a thousand such enchantments. Mind has its blissful islands as well as its mountains, its deeps, and its treacherous crossroads. Depicting these trials by horror and by enchantment, Romanticism is genuinely a rebirth of Romance.

In the years following World War I it became customary to see Classicism and Romanticism as two radically different philosophies of life and to place modernism on the side of the anti-romantic. André Malraux defined the classical element in modern art as a "lucid horror of seduction." Today it is clear that Romantic art shared that lucidity. Romanticism at its most profound reveals the depth of the enchantments in which we live. We dream, we wake on the cold hillside, and our sole self pursues the dream once more. In the beginning was the dream, and the task of disenchantment never ends.

The nature poetry of the Romantics is a case in point. Far from being an indulgence in dewy moments, it is the exploration of enchanted ground. The Romantic poets, like the Impressionist painters, refuse to "simplify the ghost" of nature. They begin to look steadfastly at all sensuous experience, penetrating its veils and facing its seductions. Shelley's "Mont Blanc" is not an enthusiastic nature poem but a spirit-drama in which the poet's mind seeks to release itself from an overwhelming impression and to reaffirm its autonomy vis-à-vis nature. Keats also goes far in respecting illusions without being deluded. His starting-point is the dream of nature fostered by Romance; he agrees to this as consciously as we lie down to sleep. But he intends such dreaming "beyond self" to unfold its own progressions and to wake into truth. . . .

It was Wordsworth, of course, whose poetry Keats had tried to escape by adhering to a less self-centered kind of sublimity: "Let us have the old Poets, and Robin Hood." Wordsworth had subdued poetry to the theme of nature's role in the growth of the individual mind. The dream of nature, in Wordsworth, does not lead to formal Romance but is an early, developmental step in converting the solipsistic into the sympathetic imagination. It entices the brooding soul out of itself, toward nature first, then toward humanity. Wordsworth knew the weight of self-consciousness:

> It seemed the very garments that I wore
> Preyed on my strength, and stopped the quiet stream
> Of self-forgetfulness.
> [*The Prelude* (1850), 5.294 ff.]

The wound of self is healed, however, by "unconscious intercourse" with a nature "old as creation." Nature makes the "quiet stream" flow on.

Wordsworth evokes a type of consciousness more integrated than ordinary consciousness, though deeply dependent on its early—and continuing—life in rural surroundings.

The Romantic emphasis on unconsciousness and organic form is significant in this light. *Unconsciousness* remains an ambiguous term in the Romantic and Victorian periods, referring to a state distinctly other than consciousness or simply to unselfconsciousness. The characteristic of right performance, says Carlyle in *Characteristics* (1831), is an unconsciousness—"'the healthy know not of their health, but only the sick.'" The term clearly approaches here its alternate meaning of unselfconsciousness, and it is to such statements that Mill must be indebted when he mentions the "anti-self-consciousness theory" of Carlyle. In America, Thoreau perpetuates the ambiguity. He also prescribes unconsciousness for his sophisticated age and uses the word as an equivalent of vision: "the absence of the speaker from his speech." It does seem to me that the personal and expressive theory of poetry, ascribed to the Romantics, and the impersonal theory of poetry, claimed in reaction by the moderns, answer to the same problem and are quietly linked by the ambiguity in *unconsciousness.* Both theories value art as thought recreated into feeling or self-consciousness into a more communal power of vision. Yet can the modern poet, whom Schiller called "sentimental" (reflective) and whom we would describe as alienated, achieve the immediacy of all great verse, whatever its personal or historical dilemma?

This is as crucial a matter today as when Wordsworth and Coleridge wrote *Lyrical Ballads* and Hölderlin pondered the fate of poetry in "Der Rhein." Is visionary poetry a thing of the past, or can it coexist with the modern temper? Is it an archaic revelation, or a universal mode springing from every real contact with nature? "To interest or benefit us," says a Victorian writer, "poetry must be reflective, sentimental, subjective; it must accord with the conscious, analytical spirit of present men." The difficulties surrounding a modern poetry of vision vary with each national literature. In England the loss of "poesy" is attributed by most Romantics to a historical though not irreversible fact—to the preceding century's infidelity to the line of Chaucer, Spenser, Shakespeare, and Milton. "Let us have the old Poets, and Robin Hood," as Keats said. Yet for the German and the French there was no easy return to a tradition deriving its strength from both learned and popular sources. "How much further along we would be," Herder remarks, "if we had used popular beliefs and myths like the British, if our poetry had built upon them as wholeheartedly as Chaucer, Spenser and Shakespeare did." In the absence of this English kind of literary mediation, the gap between medieval romance and the modern spirit seemed too great. Goethe's *Faust* tried to bridge it but, like *Wilhelm Meister,* anticipated a new type of literature which subsumed the philosophical character of the age and merged myth and irony into a "progressive" mode. The future belonged to the analytic spirit, to irony, to prose. The death of poetry had certainly occurred to the Romantics in idea, and Hegel's prediction of it was simply the overt expression of their own despair. Yet against this despair the greater Romantic poets staked their art and often their sanity.

*   *   *

Shelley's poem addresses the redemptive quality that Coleridge called joy. It is that kind of vision that makes the common become divine, the ordinary, special. Without it, death and time control life, making it a "dark reality." Shelley, unlike Coleridge, seems to consider this Power to have an existence separate from human consciousness, yet he does not associate it with another "sublimer" world. But when one is visited by it, one receives inspiration and hope.

HYMN TO INTELLECTUAL BEAUTY

Percy Bysshe Shelley (1792–1822)

I

The awful shadow of some unseen Power
    Floats though unseen among us,—visiting
  This various world with as inconstant wing
As summer winds that creep from flower to flower,—
Like moonbeams that behind some piny mountain shower,   5
    It visits with inconstant glance
    Each human heart and countenance;
Like hues and harmonies of evening,—
    Like clouds in starlight widely spread,—
    Like memory of music fled.—   10
    Like aught that for its grace may be
Dear, and yet dearer for its mystery.

II

Spirit of BEAUTY, that dost consecrate
  With thine own hues all thou dost shine upon
  Of human thought or form,—where art thou gone?   15
Why dost thou pass away and leave our state,
This dim vast vale of tears, vacant and desolate?
    Ask why the sunlight not for ever
    Weaves rainbows o'er yon mountain-river,

Why aught should fail and fade that once is shown,   20
    Why fear and dream and death and birth
    Cast on the daylight of this earth
    Such gloom,—why man has such a scope
For love and hate, despondency and hope?

III

No voice from some sublimer world hath ever   25
    To sage or poet these responses° given—
    Therefore the names of Demon, Ghost, and Heaven,
Remain the records of their vain endeavour,
Frail spells—whose uttered charm might not avail to sever,
    From all we hear and all we see,   30
    Doubt, chance, and mutability.
Thy light alone—like mist o'er mountains driven,
    Or music by the night-wind sent
    Through strings of some still instrument,
    Or moonlight on a midnight stream,   35
Gives grace and truth to life's unquiet dream.

IV

Love, Hope, and Self-esteem, like clouds depart
    And come, for some uncertain moments lent.
    Man were immortal, and omnipotent,
Didst thou, unknown and awful as thou art,   40
Keep with thy glorious train firm state within his heart.
    Thou messenger of sympathies,
    That wax and wane in lovers' eyes—
Thou—that to human thought art nourishment,
    Like darkness to a dying flame!   45
    Depart not as thy shadow came,
    Depart not—lest the grave should be,
Like life and fear, a dark reality.

V

While yet a boy I sought for ghosts, and sped
    Through many a listening chamber, cave and ruin, .   50
    And starlight wood, with fearful steps pursuing
Hopes of high talk with the departed dead.
I called on poisonous names° with which our youth is fed;

°*responses:*   answers to the questions of stanza II   °*names:*   God and Christ

I was not heard—I saw them not—
　When musing deeply on the lot　　　　　　　　　　55
Of life, at that sweet time when winds are wooing
　All vital things that wake to bring
　News of birds and blossoming,—
　　Sudden, thy shadow fell on me;
I shrieked, and clasped my hands in ecstasy!　　　　60

VI

I vowed that I would dedicate my powers
　To thee and thine—have I not kept the vow?
　With beating heart and streaming eyes, even now
I call the phantoms of a thousand hours
Each from his voiceless grave: They have in visioned bowers　　65
　Of studious zeal or love's delight
　Outwatched with me the envious night—
They know that never joy illumed my brow
　Unlinked with hope that thou wouldst free
　This world from its dark slavery,　　　　　　　70
　　That thou—O awful LOVELINESS,
Wouldst give whate'er these words cannot express.

VII

The day becomes more solemn and serene
　When noon is past—there is a harmony
　In autumn, and a lustre in its sky,　　　　　　75
Which through the summer is not heard or seen,
As if it could not be, as if it had not been!
　　Thus let thy power, which like the truth
　　Of nature on my passive youth
Descended, to my onward life supply　　　　　　80
　Its calm—to one who worships thee,
　And every form containing thee,
　　Whom, SPIRIT fair, thy spells did bind
To fear° himself, and love all human kind.

*　　*　　*

The famous poem that follows is of the kind described earlier in the
essay by Geoffrey Hartman in which the poet visits a scene of his past and

°*fear:*　revere

takes the occasion for a reflection on his own process of growth and change and the insights he has gained therefrom. For Wordsworth the achievement of sympathy seems much more derived from outward forms of Nature than for Shelley or Coleridge, but the purpose or outcome is still the establishment of a redemptive view of human experience.

LINES COMPOSED A FEW MILES ABOVE TINTERN ABBEY, ON REVISITING THE BANKS OF THE WYE DURING A TOUR. JULY 13, 1798

William Wordsworth (1770–1850)

Five years have past, five summers, with the length
Of five long winters! and again I hear
These waters,° rolling from their mountain-springs
With a soft inland murmur.—Once again
Do I behold these steep and lofty cliffs,   5
That on a wild secluded scene impress
Thoughts of more deep seclusion; and connect
The landscape with the quiet of the sky.
The day is come when I again repose
Here, under this dark sycamore, and view   10
These plots of cottage-ground, these orchard-tufts,
Which at this season, with their unripe fruits,
Are clad in one green hue, and lose themselves
'Mid groves and copses. Once again I see
These hedge-rows, hardly hedge-rows, little lines   15
Of sportive wood run wild: these pastoral farms,
Green to the very door; and wreaths of smoke
Sent up, in silence, from among the trees!
With some uncertain notice, as might seem
Of vagrant dwellers in the houseless woods,   20
Or of some Hermit's cave, where by his fire
The Hermit sits alone.
          These beauteous forms,
Through a long absence, have not been to me
As is a landscape to a blind man's eye:
But oft, in lonely rooms, and 'mid the din   25
Of towns and cities, I have owed to them
In hours of weariness, sensations sweet,
Felt in the blood, and felt along the heart;
And passing even into my purer mind,   30
With tranquil restoration:—feelings too

°*waters:* the Wye River

Of unremembered pleasure: such, perhaps,
As have no slight or trivial influence
On that best portion of a good man's life,
His little, nameless, unremembered, acts   35
Of kindness and of love. Nor less, I trust,
To them I may have owed another gift,
Of aspect more sublime; that blessed mood,
In which the burthen of the mystery,
In which the heavy and the weary weight   40
Of all this unintelligible world,
Is lightened: — that serene and blessed mood,
In which the affections gently lead us on, —
Until, the breath of this corporeal frame
And even the motion of our human blood   45
Almost suspended, we are laid asleep
In body, and become a living soul:
While with an eye made quiet by the power
Of harmony, and the deep power of joy,
We see into the life of things.   50
                    If this
Be but a vain belief, yet, oh! how oft —
In darkness and amid the many shapes
Of joyless daylight; when the fretful stir
Unprofitable, and the fever of the world,   55
Have hung upon the beatings of my heart —
How oft, in spirit, have I turned to thee,
O sylvan Wye! thou wanderer thro' the woods,
How often has my spirit turned to thee!
    And now, with gleams of half-extinguished thought   60
With many recognitions dim and faint,
And somewhat of a sad perplexity,
The picture of the mind revives again:
While here I stand, not only with the sense
Of present pleasure, but with pleasing thoughts   65
That in this moment there is life and food
For future years. And so I dare to hope,
Though changed, no doubt, from what I was when first
I came among these hills; when like a roe
I bounded o'er the mountains, by the sides   70
Of the deep rivers, and the lonely streams,
Wherever nature led: more like a man
Flying from something that he dreads, than one
Who sought the thing he loved. For nature then
(The coarser pleasures of my boyish days,   75
And their glad animal movements all gone by)

To me was all in all.—I cannot paint
What then I was. The sounding cataract
Haunted me like a passion: the tall rock,
The mountain, and the deep and gloomy wood,   80
Their colours and their forms, were then to me
An appetite; a feeling and a love,
That had no need of a remoter charm,
By thought supplied, nor any interest
Unborrowed from the eye.—That time is past,   85
And all its aching joys are now no more,
And all its dizzy raptures. Not for this
Faint I, nor mourn nor murmur; other gifts
Have followed; for such loss, I would believe,
Abundant recompense. For I have learned   90
To look on nature, not as in the hour
Of thoughtless youth; but hearing oftentimes
The still, sad music of humanity,
Nor harsh nor grating, though of ample power
To chasten and subdue. And I have felt   95
A presence that disturbs me with the joy
Of elevated thoughts; a sense sublime
Of something far more deeply interfused,
Whose dwelling is the light of setting suns,
And the round ocean and the living air,   100
And the blue sky, and in the mind of man:
A motion and a spirit, that impels
All thinking things, all objects of all thought,
And rolls through all things. Therefore am I still
A lover of the meadows and the woods,   105
And mountains; and of all that we behold
From this green earth; of all the mighty world
Of eye, and ear,—both what they half create,
And what perceive; well pleased to recognise
In nature and the language of the sense   110
The anchor of my purest thoughts, the nurse,
The guide, the guardian of my heart, and soul
Of all my moral being.
                        Nor perchance,
If I were not thus taught, should I the more   115
Suffer my genial° spirits to decay:
For thou art with me here upon the banks
Of this fair river; thou my dearest Friend,
My dear, dear Friend; and in thy voice I catch

°*genial:* inborn, native

The language of my former heart, and read   120
My former pleasures in the shooting lights
Of thy wild eyes. Oh! yet a little while
May I behold in thee what I was once,
My dear, dear Sister! and this prayer I make,
Knowing that Nature never did betray   125
The heart that loved her; 'tis her privilege,
Through all the years of this our life, to lead
From joy to joy: for she can so inform
The mind that is within us, so impress
With quietness and beauty, and so feed   130
With lofty thoughts, that neither evil tongues,
Rash judgments, nor the sneers of selfish men,
Nor greetings where no kindness is, nor all
The dreary intercourse of daily life,
Shall e'er prevail against us, or disturb   135
Our cheerful faith, that all which we behold
Is full of blessings. Therefore let the moon
Shine on thee in thy solitary walk;
And let the misty mountain-winds be free
To blow against thee: and, in after years,   140
When these wild ecstasies shall be matured
Into a sober pleasure; when thy mind
Shall be a mansion for all lovely forms,
Thy memory be as a dwelling-place
For all sweet sounds and harmonies; oh! then,   145
If solitude, or fear, or pain, or grief,
Should be thy portion, with what healing thoughts
Of tender joy wilt thou remember me,
And these my exhortations! Nor, perchance—
If I should be where I no more can hear   150
Thy voice, nor catch from thy wild eyes these gleams
Of past existence—wilt thou then forget
That on the banks of this delightful stream
We stood together; and that I, so long
A worshipper of Nature, hither came   155
Unwearied in that service: rather say
With warmer love—oh! with far deeper zeal
Of holier love. Nor wilt thou then forget
That after many wanderings, many years   160
Of absence, these steep woods and lofty cliffs,
And this green pastoral landscape, were to me
More dear, both for themselves and for thy sake!

*   *   *

QUESTIONS

1. What are the strengths and weaknesses implied in Whitman's spider metaphor? What is the cause of the Soul's isolation? What are the primary attributes of the spider?

2. Think of other natural phenomena that might present the idea of isolation and its effects — and its being overcome. Where in Nature does one find the energies making connections between things?

3. In "Dejection: An Ode," Stanza I: What is the condition of weather as the poem begins? Why does the speaker quote from the old ballad as a source of forecasting? Where in the stanza does the speaker give a name to his state of mind? What has this to do with the moon and the Aeolian lute? What element of his state of mind do you recognize as part of the Romantic problem? What does "wonted" mean?

4. In Stanza II: What adjectives does the speaker apply to his "mood"? How long has he been feeling it? What has he been trying to do about it? What is his initial explanation of what is wrong?

5. In Stanza III: What further insight does the speaker achieve in this stanza? What is the effect of this gradual process of insight? Why did he not see this at first? What clues did he have along the way? Where did his grasp of his difficulty make the greatest improvement?

6. In Stanza IV: What is the figure by which the speaker speaks of the relationships between man and Nature? What does the soul produce? What motion is in its production? What does the soul's effort accomplish? Why, if he knows what is required, does he not succeed in changing his state of mind?

7. In Stanza V: There are two important images in this stanza: the luminous mist and the wedding garment of stanza II. How does the choice of these images contribute to the idea of Joy? What is the value of a "Wedding" with Nature? Give a serious account of what this idea means. Why can the sensual and proud not know about this? Who can experience joy? Line 72 is a summary of the idea. Comment on it. How is this different from pride?

8. In Stanza VI: What are the contrasts between the joy the Lady feels and the joy which a happy man feels, and the happiness described in this stanza? What is the history of his present dejection? How is it like the dark night of the soul? What did Nature give that he had lost?

9. In Stanza VII: What has happened to the weather? Explain why Coleridge uses these changes in the weather in a poem about psychological difficulties. What view of Nature is now suggested? What season of the year is it? What fanciful visions does the wind suggest? Do these seem likely to supply a remedy for the dejection? Why or why not?

10. In Stanza VIII: What achievement does the author have at the end of the poem? How is he better off than at the beginning? How has he

not changed? What problems remain? What definition of Redemption does the poem offer?

11. What stages does the Mariner's journey contain? What is the problem he faces at various points? What are the major turning points in his voyage? What events or circumstances lead to change?

12. Look carefully at the aspects of Nature which the Mariner encounters: the Wind, the Lack of Wind, Rain, Sun, Moon, Stars, Heat, Cold, and Sea Water. What events in the voyage are connected with natural events?

13. The Albatross and the Water Snakes, air and water creatures, are important to the Mariner. What attitude does he take toward these creatures? What attitude do the shipmates take?

14. As a Quest Narrative, what is the Mariner seeking? What is the "purpose" of his voyage? How would the meaning be different if the journey had taken place on land instead of sea?

15. What does Coleridge do to direct the reader's attention away from literal interpretation? What is the effect of having the Mariner tell his story to passersby? Why, in this case, a Wedding Guest?

16. The marginal gloss, the intentionally antique language, the simple ballad meter are striking contrivances of Coleridge. What is his purpose in the use of these devices?

17. Coleridge told an acquaintance that he was afraid that the poem "had too much moral." What could he have meant by this remark?

18. What are the signs of Redemption? How are they achieved and how maintained?

19. What is the connection Hartman sees between Self-Consciousness and the story of the expulsion from Eden?

20. How can poetry, myth, and religion defend the mind against itself?

21. How do "wandering" and "revisiting" aid the redemptive process?

22. How do Romantic poets, in Hartman's view, use Nature? How does this use contrast with the usual idea of Romantic indulgence in admiration of Nature?

23. What do Shelley's and Wordsworth's poems have in common? What do they see as blighting human life, and what do they see as offering joy and hope?

24. What techniques do these poets use to overcome Self-Consciousness? Which seems to be the more successful, the more appealing?

25. Which form of Redemption seems most convincing and most easy to acquire? Explain.

26. Compare the role of Nature in these two poems with that in "Dejection: An Ode."

PART V

Some Romantic Ideas

Some Romantic Ideas

Self and Reality

Of all the changes in the point of view that separate the 18th century from the 19th, the Traditional from the Romantic, one of the most important was the loss of confidence that Romantics felt in the validity of the usual judgments of Reality offered by science. The Romantics discovered, or came to feel, that to some degree all perceptions are subjective, are functions of the observer, that what is seen depends more on what or who is doing the seeing than on what is "out there." As William Blake puts the matter: as the eye, so the object. To the Romantic, Reality is created by the Self 's perception of it. Nothing exists until a Self thinks of it, until it is brought to reality by being made a part of Consciousness. The world of dogs and cats, of people and railway trains and shoes and ships and sealing wax, has no substance, does not count, says the Romantic, until it is conceived by a human consciousness. Reality is a Self, Seeing. I am when I think, and when I think of you, you are.

The idea of subjective influences on the act of perception is not, at one level, very surprising. We are aware that people under the weight of strong feeling often "see" things differently from more dispassionate observers: we argue the judgment of umpires and referees when they affect the fortunes of our favorite team; we disagree about the qualities of people we strongly like or dislike; we note that witnesses to events often report differently as to what happened. The Romantic simply takes this idea further by saying that since each individual is unique, each Self a particular set of experience and history, then each perception an individual Self makes must be different from one made by another Self. This is the case particularly when the perceptions involve other people, ideas, values, or things of the spirit, that is, things that are most emotionally connected and often most meaningful to people. In order to know, the mind makes an effort to project its consciousness out of its isolation into the world outside, to create a relationship with an object, idea, or another person. (We see how common this idea has become when we notice the current sense of one's "relating" to another person.) In the useful figure of one historian of this doctrine, the mind to the Romantic is like a lamp, providing the light by which objects come into existence. When there is no light, there is nothing; so, when there is no mind or consciousness, there is no thing.

The contrasting view starts from the opposite side: things outside exist, absolutely. Things, objects, cats and dogs, cabbages and kings, and so forth are real, and their existence is neither created nor in need of verification by human intelligence. Accurate human intellection, it follows, consists of obtaining in the mind accurate pictures or accounts of what is out there. Accuracy in this case means getting rid of subjective influences: not what we want to see, not what our feelings wish us to know, but what is actually, truly, objectively "there." This, of course, is the objective of the scientific method, the seeing of data without bias or prejudice, even when the experiment does not come out as expected. The metaphor for mind under this system is that of a mirror: a surface that reflects accurately or imperfectly the things it sees but that has no part in making the objects. A bad reflection is a distortion, but it is blamed on the mind, not the object.

There are two ways of asserting the reality of objects under a traditional, non-Romantic system of thought. The first holds that all matter and all things are in a sense God's creation, indeed human beings and consciousness itself occur only because God wills them to occur. If He stopped so willing, existence would cease in an instant. As Plato has it, all Reality as we know it is an imitation of an Ideal that exists absolutely, prior to humanity, in some other place and time. As the Christian has it, God exists, and his Energy or Spirit creates matter, and animals, vegetables, and minerals and, last, Man and Woman, put into the world of these preexisting things to govern and use them, but not to be responsible for their making.

A similar version of this view of Reality belongs to scientists, who begin with the hypothesis that nature exists and that the enterprise of science is to learn more about it, to discover its objective patterns and character. Whether they think God created it or not, they believe that it has regularity, clarity, and a kind of symmetry, and their enterprise is to construct the best hypothesis about its regularity that they can.

In either case the essential and basic assumption of Romanticism is that Knowing is a projection of inner, personal, and subjective energies of the Self into the World; to the Traditionalist it is a submission of the mind to absolutist categories that exist prior to human experience.

So stated, of course, the issue has a simple clarity and polarity, yet we can immediately acknowledge, as the Romantics themselves did, that often one can use both modes of knowing at the same time. When one's car fails to start on the cold, wet morning on which one has an important engagement waiting, one may analyze the causes of failure by recalling diagrams of electrical circuitry and reasoning that the reality is a damp spark coil that is causing ignition failure and can be remedied by a careful effort to dry the coil. At the same time, one may feel that the machine is evil, one may utter hostile words about auto manufacturers, about the weather, and if one is more philosophical, the fates. It is clear, however, that both responses to this situation are true, that both have a measure of reality, and that the mind is quite capable of doing two things at once — of cursing the fates and drying the spark coil.

Because intelligent people can operate in two modes of mentality at the same time, Romanticism should not be equated with simple anti-rationality. It is not a point of view that scoffs at science and deduction. Many Romantic writers were intensely interested in science, and were not foolish enough to think they could get their cars started by creating, out of their own consciousness, a dry spark plug. But what they did feel was that there was an essential difference in kind between subjective and objective knowledge, that to most men a good deal of the time the subjective view is more important, and more truthful. Such a view does indeed place Science and Rationality lower on a scale of value than Feeling and Imagination; however it does not say that Reason is to be disregarded.

Insofar as Romanticism was historically opposed to science it was to the exaggerated claims of science, to the application of scientific method in the social sciences to all human conditions and institutions and to the excesses and unhappiness in human terms that a denial of feeling, a too-intense use of Reason may bring. These sufferings have already been considered in Part III.

Because reality is interior and subjective, occurring in the encounter of the Self with Others, Romantic art will commonly be expressive of Inner Reality or, to put it simply, of a state of feeling. It will try to *be* the moment of Encounter. It will not care to *imitate* or *mirror* external things because, in this belief, those external things have no absolute reality. Moreover, because feeling is transitory, moving in time, developing, evolving, changing, then the feeling of the moment is not the same as the feeling of the next moment, any more than the feeling one person has on a given occasion or in a given experience is the same as the feeling another person might have. In short, because all experience is relative to the subjective experience of the experiencer, then all art is particularized, is the special particular statement or expression of a state of feeling. It does not claim objective judgments, it does not claim Truths in any large general sense. Moreover, it tries to bring us the first-hand, real movement of experience, the things of the mind's encounter, in the dramatic and immediate form in which they occur. Romantic poetry, therefore, has as its natural form the lyric poem, the poem in which the appearance of natural, spontaneous expression is striven for, in which the poet is, as it were, overheard, the poem in which powerful feeling—in a favorite Romantic metaphor—overflows as naturally and unrehearsedly as a fountain falls over the brim of its pool.

Such ease, as anyone who has ever tried poetry or any other kind of creative thought will know, is rarely accomplished, so we must admit that the Romantic mode of poetry is one of the convention of spontaneity, the contrivance of a poem that looks or sounds as if it lacked forethought, as if it did not require care, revision, editing, and other unspontaneous emendations.

Because we are always asked to hear a genuine feeling, to recognize and respond to the quality of sincerity or authenticity in the speech, the key to analysis of the lyric poem is a notice of the Voice, the particular human condition, the special attributes of the speaker of a particular poem. Romantic poets put great store, therefore, in the personal style, the mode of expression that captures the sincerity of the feeling, the honest qualities of the emotion that gives rise to the poem. The degree and quality and amount of that direct sincerity is often a key to recognition of Romantic art, and the lyric form, which is the primary mode of Romantic poetry, has reached brilliant development in the hands of the most substantial Romantic writers.

The lyric, of course, is always short. As Coleridge was the first to observe, by this definition there can be no long Romantic poems—only shorter lyric moments connected by passages of another kind. Compared to the traditional forms of literary expression—the epic, the narrative, and the imitation of models from the past—the lyric is short, sweet, carried forward out of the consciousness of the poet by its own energy, and then expiring like breath or a spark as the feeling it expresses is fulfilled or satisfied.

*   *   *

From ROMANTICISM AS A MODERN TRADITION

Robert Langbaum (1924–   )

Once we understand that we are interested in Romanticism not as a recurring phenomenon but as that movement in thought and art which followed the eighteenth century, it is not difficult to agree, in defining Romanticism, on those qualities which could have occurred only after the eighteenth century. Nor is it difficult to account for most of those qualities as determined by the attempt to answer the central question posed by the Enlightenment—the question of tradition, of how, after the collapse of the traditional authority for values, to find and justify new values. It is when we think of Romanticism as being an attempt to answer this question or as being in large measure literature's answer to science, that we can understand it as being essentially a doctrine of experience, an attempt to salvage on science's own empirical ground the validity of the individual perception against scientific abstractions.

From *The Poetry of Experience,* by Robert Langbaum. Copyright © 1957 by Robert Langbaum. Reprinted by permission of Random House, Inc.

The advantage of understanding Romanticism in its post-Enlightenment character as a doctrine of experience is that we understand it as the movement which unites us to the 19th century instead of separating us from it. For we are still children of the Enlightenment. We are still trying to mark out a path through the wilderness bequeathed us by the Enlightenment; we are still seeking values in a world in which neither tradition nor science offers much assistance to that end. If anything, the wilderness has grown wilder since the 19th century. Time, two world wars, and universal social upheaval have removed us even farther from the traditional past and the spread of technological culture has given science an increasing dominion over our lives. To bridge the increased gap between knowledge and value, we ought to require, if our reasoning thus far has been correct, an even more extreme and articulated Romanticism. The question even arises whether, in the post-Enlightenment world, in a scientific and democratic age, literature, whatever its program, can be anything but Romantic in the sense I mean. . . .

In making their new kind of poetry, many romanticists announced that they were sacrificing form in the interest of *sincerity*. They announced an ideal of artlessness—Coleridge finding the perfect poet in the eolian harp which, being played on by the wind, makes music without intervention of art, Shelley finding him in the skylark which pours out its

> full heart
> In profuse strains of unpremeditated art,

Faust teaching the pedantic classicist, Wagner, that sincerity is the only effective rhetoric:

> but you'll never move others, heart to heart,
> unless your speech comes from your own heart.

Yet the anti-rhetorical style is itself a rhetoric. For there remains, between the sincere feeling in the heart and the effect of sincerity on the page, the art of communication. Literary scholarship has by now discounted the popular illusion that the best romantic poetry sprang full-blown from the poet's heart, unrevised and unlabored (that the illusion existed is a sign of the success of the romantic rhetoric). The point, therefore, in understanding the form of romantic poetry is to understand how the sincere, unpremeditated effect is achieved—the history of romanticism being largely the history of the attempt of the poets and critics to arrive at that understanding. . . .

We would therefore require, to talk intelligently about the form of romantic poetry, a theory which could account for both the artlessness and the artifice, the sincerity and the insincerity, the subjectivity and the objectivity, of poetry since the Enlightenment. We would require, in other words, a theory to connect the poetry of the nineteenth and twentieth centuries, to connect romanticism with the so-called reactions against it. We are now in a position to advance such a theory. For having seen the poetry which set out to be different from romantic poetry, we can find in the core that remains unchanged the essential idea of romanticism. That essential idea is, I would suggest, the doctrine of experience—the doctrine that the imaginative apprehension gained through immediate experience is primary and certain, whereas the analytic reflection that follows is secondary and problematical. The poetry of the nineteenth and twentieth centuries can thus be seen in connection as a poetry of experience—a poetry constructed upon the deliberate disequilibrium between experience and idea, a poetry which makes its statement not as an idea but as an experience from which one or more ideas can be abstracted as problematical rationalizations.

Much could be learned from the isolation of a poetry of experience. It would reveal for the first time, in addition to the distinctively romantic sensibility and subject matter which we already know, a distinctively romantic form in poetry—a form of which the potentials are realized in the so-called reactions against romantic poetry, in the dramatic monologues of the Victorians, and the symbolist poems of the moderns. Such a form, furthermore, if it were treated as a way of meaning, a way of establishing the validity of a poetic statement, would become the best index of a distinctively modern tradition. What better sign can there be, after all, of a culture's real belief than the principle by which it establishes the validity of its statements of values? And what better sign can there be of its coherence than the fact that it can make such statements, statements combining its unspoken convictions on the nature of truth, goodness and beauty? Form is a better index of a tradition than a subject matter, in that subject matter is often controversial; it is often an index of what people think they believe, whereas form is an index of what is believed too implicitly to be discussed.

Since a new culture, like a new art, looks disorderly until we discover its principle of order, and since the principle which gives order to a culture is intimately related to the principle which gives order to its art, the critic who finds the latter principle is by implication at least helping to find the former. If in addition to isolating the poetry of experience as a form, as a way of establishing in an anti-dogmatic and empiricist age a truth based on the disequilibrium between experience and idea, he could show that there emerges from this deliberate disequilibrium a correspondingly new moral and aesthetic symmetry—he would have suggested at least one line of coherence by which to discern in the bewildering heterogeneity of modern culture a distinctively modern tradition. Such a tradition would present a curious paradox in that it would have been created out of the rejection of tradition and the preoccupation with its loss. We would find that the artists and thinkers of the last one hundred and seventy-five years or so have, in proclaiming the freedom of modern life, actually laid down new rules for it, that they have, in proclaiming its meaninglessness and disunity, formulated for it a new meaning and a new unity.

*   *   *

Time and Process

One of the most difficult and yet important Romantic ideas is that all organic processes—the life of a cell, the life of a human being, the life of any given species or form of plant or animal—is lived in time. There are many consequences to this idea, but the most obvious is this: no truth, no state of mind, no value, no condition of life can be looked on as fixed or permanent. Mutability, as the Renaissance poets called it, the liability of all living matter to change, to movement, and ultimately to extinction, must color and shade each moment of life.

Romantic metaphysics requires that we must learn to live as well and as happily as we can within this constant movement of time, within the ever-changing consciousness that mind and emotions contain. We must have the strength and learn the wisdom to avoid reliance on absolute categories of scientific truth and value and not to depend on fixed quantities. We must make anew each experience, see each new moment as offering and requiring a new synthesis, a new evaluation. We are always different today from yesterday, and different too, however slightly, from what we will be tomorrow, by which time one more set of experiences (today's) will have been added to our personal and unique history. Blake's little verse summarizes this difficult point:

> He who binds to himself a joy
> Does the wingèd life destroy;
> But he who kisses the joy as it flies
> Lives in eternity's sun rise.

To paraphrase Blake's view: only when we can live what we would now call existentially, accepting and affirming the motions of time and our will within time, can we escape the pains and sorrow that awareness of time brings. When we try to escape time by denying change, by fixing our attention on things we like, by trying to hold on to the moment for its joy, we deny by that very act the positive character of movement and the essential nature of our own consciousness, which are in time and are violated by our attempts to identify with fixity and absolutism.

This is not an easy idea to grasp, even in these abstract terms and formulations, let alone in one's real existence. To the Romantic, life is an encounter of the Romantic Spirit with the Fixed, the Static, the Timeless. It is an encounter between Life and Death, between the forces of Movement, Energy, and Creativity with the opposite forces of entropy, darkness, and cold.

There are a number of important consequences of the Romantic perception of this idea. One of the most vexing yet suggestive is this: If all life is movement, a passage from birth to death, a part of some larger movement that involves all other organic forms and perhaps even the universe itself, what is the purpose of all this movement, either local or universal? If there is no End, how can there be Purpose?

The selections in Part V offer two "answers" to these questions. Both are in one sense mystical, going beyond science, drawing on experience and feeling. The first selection is drawn from anthropology. Its content may be stated in simple terms: what we see in the history of organic life on the earth is movement. That movement has been for the most part a movement from what we call lower to what we call higher forms, from simple, single-celled organisms to vast complexities, millions of cells, organized in millions of different ways. This process of change has occurred over billions of years on this earth and perhaps even longer elsewhere. The Romantic question Eiseley considers is "Why?". What is the purpose of this Process? Where, if anywhere, is it going? Is it only Movement, or is it Direction? What, if any, is its End?

These are cosmic speculations to which there are perhaps two broad categories of answer. One is to say that there is no purpose, that the processes of organic life in the universe are governed by the interaction of the specific chemical processes of the life forms with the environment. The human mind is a particular event in that huge process, but its emergence from the simpler cellular forms has no absolute value or meaning beyond that which we confer on ourselves and our Consciousness of Ourselves.

A second answer is that the process does have a direction, a *telos*, an End higher than the beginning, that End being somehow inherent in the process. Human consciousness is evolving from and to by means of an energy or force or spirit in matter that "knows" this End and by some means produces the process.

*　　*　　*

Loren Eiseley, anthropologist, biologist, naturalist, philosopher, and humanist, thought about the meanings of biological facts and their relation to human understanding. His speculations on one of the critical moments in the History of Process are given in the following essay from *The Immense Journey*.

THE SNOUT

Loren Eiseley (1907–1977)

I have long been an admirer of the octopus. The cephalopods are very old, and they have slipped, protean, through many shapes. They are the wisest of the mollusks, and I have always felt it to be just as well for us that they never came ashore, but—there are other things that have.

There is no need to be frightened. It is true some of the creatures are odd, but I find the situation rather heartening than otherwise. It gives one a feeling of confidence to see nature still busy with experiments, still dynamic, and not through nor satisfied because a Devonian fish managed to end as a two-legged character with a straw hat. There are other things brewing and growing in the oceanic vat. It pays to know this. It pays to know there is just as much future as there is past. The only thing that doesn't pay is to be sure of man's own part in it.

There are things down there still coming ashore. Never make the mistake of thinking life is now adjusted for eternity. It gets into your head—the certainty, I mean—the human certainty, and then you miss it all: the things on the tide flats and what they mean, and why, as my wife says, "they ought to be watched."

The trouble is we don't know what to watch for. I have a friend, one of these Explorers Club people, who drops in now and then between trips to tell me about the size of crocodile jaws in Uganda, or what happened on some back beach in Arnhem Land.

"They fell out of the trees," he said. "Like rain. And into the boat."

"Uh?" I said, noncommittally.

"They did *so*," he protested, "and they were hard to catch."

"Really—" I said.

"We were pushing a dugout up one of the tidal creeks in northern Australia and going fast when *smacko* we jam this mangrove bush and the things come tumbling down.

"What were they doing sitting up there in bunches? I ask you. It's no place for a fish. Besides that they had a way of sidling off with those popeyes trained on you. I never liked it. Somebody ought to keep an eye on them."

"Why?" I asked.

"I don't know why," he said impatiently, running a rough, square hand through his hair and wrinkling his forehead. "I just mean they make you feel that way, is all. A fish belongs in the water. It ought to stay there—just as we live on land in houses. Things ought to know their place and stay in it, but those fish have got a way of sidling off. As though they had mental reservations and weren't keeping any contracts. See what I mean?"

"I see what you mean," I said gravely. "They ought to be watched. My wife thinks so too. About a lot of things."

"She does?" He brightened. "Then that's two of us. I don't know why, but they give you that feeling."

He didn't know why, but I thought that I did.

It began as such things always begin—in the ooze of unnoticed swamps, in the darkness of eclipsed moons. It began with a strangled gasping for air.

The pond was a place of reek and corruption, of fetid smells and of oxygen-starved fish breathing through laboring gills. At times the slowly contracting circle of the water left little windrows of minnows who skittered desperately to escape the sun, but who died, nevertheless, in the fat, warm mud. It was a place of low life. In it the human brain began.

There were strange snouts in those waters, strange barbels nuzzling the bottom ooze, and there was time—three hundred million years of it—but mostly, I think, it was the ooze. By day the temperature in the world outside the pond rose to a frightful intensity; at night the sun went down in smoking red. Dust storms marched in incessant progression across a wilderness whose plants were the plants of long ago. Leafless and weird and stiff they lingered by the water, while over vast areas of grassless uplands the winds blew until red stones took on the polish of reflecting mirrors. There was nothing to hold the land in place. Winds howled, dust clouds rolled, and brief erratic torrents choked with silt ran down to the sea. It was a time of dizzying contrasts, a time of change.

On the oily surface of the pond, from time to time a snout thrust upward, took in air with a queer grunting inspiration, and swirled back to the bottom. The pond was doomed, the water was foul, and the oxygen almost gone, but the creature would not die. It could breathe air direct through a little accessory lung, and it could walk. In all that weird and lifeless landscape, it was the only thing that could. It walked rarely and under protest, but that was not surprising. The creature was a fish.

In the passage of days the pond became a puddle, but the Snout survived. There was dew one dark night and a coolness in the empty stream bed. When the sun rose next morning the pond was an empty place of cracked mud, but the Snout did not lie there. He had gone. Down stream there were other ponds. He breathed air for a few hours and hobbled slowly along on the stumps of heavy fins.

It was an uncanny business if there had been anyone there to see. It was a journey best not observed in daylight, it was something that needed swamps and shadows and the touch of the night dew. It was a monstrous penetration of a forbidden element, and the Snout kept his face from the light. It was just as well, though the face should not be mocked. In three hundred million years it would be our own.

There was something fermenting in the brain of the Snout. He was no longer entirely a fish. The ooze had marked him. It takes a swamp-and-tide-flat zoologist to tell you about life; it is in this domain that the living suffer great extremes, it is here that the water-failures, driven to desperation, make starts in a new element. It is here that strange compromises are made and new senses are born. The Snout was no exception. Though he breathed and walked primarily in order to stay in the water, he was coming ashore.

He was not really a successful fish except that he was managing to stay alive in a noisome, uncomfortable, oxygen-starved environment. In fact the time was coming when the last of his kind, harried by more ferocious and speedier fishes, would slip off the edge of the continental shelf, to seek safety in the sunless abysses of the deep sea. But the Snout was a fresh-water Crossopterygian, to give him his true name, and cumbersome and plodding though he was, something had happened back of his eyes. The ooze had gotten in its work.

It is interesting to consider what sort of creatures we, the remote descendants of the Snout, might be, except for that green quagmire out of which he came. Mammalian insects perhaps we should have been — solid-brained, our neurones wired for mechanical responses, our lives running out with the perfection of beautiful, intricate, and mindless clocks. More likely we should never have existed at all. It was the Snout and the ooze that did it. Perhaps there also, among rotting fish heads and blue, night-burning bog lights, moved the eternal mystery, the careful finger of God. The increase was not much. It was two bubbles, two thin-walled little balloons at the end of the Snout's small brain. The cerebral hemispheres had appeared.

Among all the experiments in that dripping, ooze-filled world, one was vital: the brain had to be fed. The nerve tissues are insatiable devourers of oxygen. If they do not get it, life is gone. In stagnant swamp waters, only the development of a highly efficient blood supply to the brain can prevent disaster. And among those gasping, dying creatures, whose small brains winked out forever in the long Silurian drought, the Snout and his brethren survived.

Over the exterior surface of the Snout's tiny brain ran the myriad blood vessels that served it; through the greatly enlarged choroid plexuses, other vessels pumped oxygen into the spinal fluid. The brain was a thin-walled tube fed from both surfaces. It could only exist as a thing of thin walls permeated with oxygen. To thicken, to lay down solid masses of nervous tissue such as exist among the fishes in oxygenated waters was to invite disaster. The Snout lived on a bubble, two bubbles in his brain.

It was not that his thinking was deep; it was only that it had to be thin. The little bubbles of the hemispheres helped to spread the area upon which higher correlation centers could be built, and yet preserve those areas from the disastrous thickenings which meant oxygen death to the swamp dweller. There is a mystery about those thickenings which culminate in the so-called solid brain. It is the brain of insects, of the modern fishes, of some reptiles and all birds. Always it marks the appearance of elaborate patterns of instinct and the end of thought. A road has been taken which, anatomically, is well-nigh irretraceable; it does not lead in the direction of a high order of consciousness.

Wherever, instead, the thin sheets of gray matter expand upward into the enormous hemispheres of the human brain, laughter, or it may be sorrow, enters in. Out of the choked Devonian waters emerged sight and sound and the music that rolls invisible through the composer's brain. They are there still in the ooze along the tideline, though no one notices. The world is fixed, we say: fish in the sea, birds in the air. But in the mangrove swamps by the Niger, fish climb trees and ogle uneasy naturalists who try unsuccessfully to chase them back to the water. There are things still coming ashore.

The door to the past is a strange door. It swings open and things pass through it, but they pass in one direction only. No man can return across that threshold, though he can look down still and see the green light waver in the water weeds.

There are two ways to seek the doorway: in the swamps of the inland waterways and along the tide flats of the estuaries where rivers come to the sea. By those two pathways life came ashore. It was not the magnificent march through the breakers and up the cliffs that we fondly imagine. It was a stealthy advance made in suffocation and terror, amidst the leaching bite of chemical discomfort. It was made by the failures of the sea.

Some creatures have slipped through the invisible chemical barrier between salt and fresh water into the tidal rivers, and later come ashore; some have crept upward from the salt. In all cases, however, the first adventure into the dreaded atmosphere seems to have been largely determined by the inexorable crowding of enemies and by the retreat further and further into marginal situations where the oxygen supply was depleted. Finally, in the ruthless selection of the swamp margins, or in the scramble for food on the tide flats, the land becomes home.

Not the least interesting feature of some of the tide-flat emergents is their definite antipathy for the full tide. It obstructs their food-collecting on the mud banks and brings their enemies. Only extremes of fright will drive them into the water for any period.

I think it was the great nineteenth-century paleontologist Cope who first clearly enunciated what he called the "law of the unspecialized," the contention that it was not from the most highly organized and dominant forms of a given geological era that the master type of a succeeding period evolved, but that instead the dominant forms tended to arise from more lowly and generalized animals which were capable of making new adaptations, and which were not narrowly restricted to a given environment.

There is considerable truth to this observation, but, for all that, the idea is not simple. Who is to say without foreknowledge of the future which animal is specialized and which is not? We have only to consider our remote ancestor, the Snout, to see the intricacies into which the law of the unspecialized may lead us.

If we had been making zoological observations in the Paleozoic Age, with no knowledge of the strange realms life was to penetrate in the future, we would probably have regarded the Snout as specialized. We would have seen his air-bladder lung, his stubby, sluggish fins, and his odd ability to wriggle overland as specialized adaptations to a peculiarly restricted environmental niche in stagnant continental waters. We would have thought in water terms and we would have dismissed the Snout as an interesting failure off the main line of progressive evolution, escaping from his enemies and surviving successfully only in the dreary and marginal surroundings scorned by the swift-finned teleost° fishes who were destined to dominate the seas and all quick waters.

Yet it was this poor specialization — this bog-trapped failure — whose descendants, in three great movements, were to dominate the earth. It is only now, looking backward, that we dare to regard him as "generalized." The Snout was the first vertebrate to pop completely through the water membrane into a new dimension. His very specializations and failures, in a water sense, had preadapted him for a world he scarcely knew existed.

The day of the Snout was over three hundred million years ago. Not long since I read a book in which a prominent scientist spoke cheerfully of some ten billion years of future time remaining to us. He pointed out happily the things that man might do throughout that period. Fish in the sea, I thought again, birds in the air. The climb all far behind us, the species fixed and sure. No wonder my explorer friend had had a momentary qualm when he met the mudskippers with their mental reservations and lack of promises. There is something wrong with our world view. It is still Ptolemaic, though the sun is no longer believed to revolve around the earth.

We teach the past, we see farther backward into time than any race before us, but we stop at the present, or, at best, we project far into the future idealized versions of ourselves. All that long way behind us we see, perhaps inevitably, through human eyes alone. We see ourselves as the culmination and the end, and if we do indeed consider our passing, we think that sunlight will go with us and the earth be dark. We are the end. For us continents rose and fell, for us the waters and the air were mastered, for us the great living web has pulsated and grown more intricate.

°*teleost:* bony

To deny this, a man once told me, is to deny God. This puzzled me. I went back along the pathway to the marsh. I went, not in the past, not by the bones of dead things, not down the lost roadway of the Snout. I went instead in daylight, in the Now, to see if the door was still there, and to see what things passed through.

I found that the same experiments were brewing, that up out of that ancient well, fins were still scrambling toward the sunlight. They were small things, and which of them presaged the future I could not say. I saw only that they were many and that they had solved the oxygen death in many marvelous ways, not always ours.

I found that there were modern fishes who breathed air, not through a lung but through their stomachs or through strange chambers where their gills should be, or breathing as the Snout once breathed. I found that some crawled in the fields at nightfall pursuing insects, or slept on the grass by pond sides and who drowned, if kept under water, as men themselves might drown.

Of all these fishes the mudskipper *Periophthalmus* is perhaps the strangest. He climbs trees with his fins and pursues insects; he snaps worms like a robin on the tide flats; he sees as land things see, and above all he dodges and evades with a curious popeyed insolence more suggestive of the land than of the sea. Of a different tribe and a different time he is, nevertheless, oddly reminiscent of the Snout.

But not the same. There lies the hope of life. The old ways are exploited and remain, but new things come, new senses try the unfamiliar air. There are small scuttlings and splashings in the dark, and out of it come the first croaking, illiterate voices of the things to be, just as man once croaked and dreamed darkly in that tiny vesicular forebrain.

Perpetually, now, we search and bicker and disagree. The eternal form eludes us—the shape we conceive as ours. Perhaps the old road through the marsh should tell us. We are one of many appearances of the thing called Life; we are not its perfect image, for it has no image except Life, and life is multitudinous and emergent in the stream of time.

*   *   *

The idea of Time and Process may also apply to individuals. The struggle from sea to land, from water to air, has its analogies in the aspirations of life, in the growth of youth toward adulthood, of ignorance toward knowledge, of potential toward achievement. The energy or Force of this process is perhaps the same as impelled the Snout. We see it also in the song of Barth's individual and intimate Night Voyager as it aspires toward something new and different, asking as it goes the same teleological questions as were inarticulately represented by the flopping migration of the Snout.

John Barth dramatizes that process by attributing an ironical, skeptical, and humorous consciousness and voice to a human spermatozoon as it swims along with several hundred million brother spermatozoa upward in a night-sea journey toward some Other, some different condition, toward a Destiny to which it dimly but articulately aspires, speculating as it goes on the source or the energy that drives it and on the meaning or purpose that it is enacting.

Barth's purposes in this story are both common and broad. On the one hand the Voice represents a simple biological process of conception of the kind that has occurred in the history of all living matter, the process of sexual reproduction. At another level the Voice is that of the artist. What the Artist transmits is the Tradition of Ideas and values that Art contains and that is kept alive in time through the Artist's work that survives time. Finally, the voice debates the philosophic question of the Origins of Life: who is our "Maker," or proper "Parent," and what is his relation to us, once we have been created?

From LOST IN THE FUNHOUSE

John Barth (1931–)

NIGHT-SEA JOURNEY

"One way or another, no matter which theory of our journey is correct, it's myself I address; to whom I rehearse as to a stranger our history and condition, and will disclose my secret hope though I sink for it.

"Is the journey my invention? Do the night, the sea, exist at all, I ask myself, apart from my experience of them? Do I myself exist, or is this a dream? Sometimes I wonder. And if I am, who am I? The Heritage° I supposedly transport? But how can I be both vessel and contents? Such are the questions that beset my intervals of rest.

"My trouble is, I lack conviction. Many accounts of our situation seem plausible to me—where and what we are, why we swim and whither. But implausible ones as well, perhaps especially those, I must admit as possibly correct. Even likely. If at times, in certain humors—stroking in unison, say, with my neighbors and chanting with them 'Onward! Upward!'—I have supposed that we have after all a common Maker,° Whose nature and motives we may not know, but Who engendered us in some mysteri-

---

°*Heritage:* The cell contains the genetic material of its "Maker" and of His Maker, and so on.   °*a common Maker:* in one sense, the father or producer of the spermatozoa; in another sense, God the Father

ous wise and launched us forth toward some end known but to Him—if (for a moodslength only) I have been able to entertain such notions, very popular in certain quarters, it is because our night-sea journey partakes of their absurdity. One might even say: I can believe them *because* they are absurd.

"Has that been said before?

"Another paradox: it appears to be these recesses from swimming that sustain me in the swim. Two measures onward and upward, flailing with the rest, then I float exhausted and dispirited, brood upon the night, the sea, the journey, while the flood bears me a measure back and down: slow progress, but I live, I live, and make my way, aye, past many a drownèd comrade in the end, stronger, worthier than I, victims of their unremitting *joie de nager.*° I have seen the best swimmers of my generation go under. Numberless the number of the dead! Thousands drown as I think this thought, millions as I rest before returning to the swim. And scores, hundreds of millions have expired since we surged forth, brave in our innocence, upon our dreadful way. 'Love! Love!' we sang then, a quarter-billion strong, and churned the warm sea white with joy of swimming! Now all are gone down—the buoyant, the sodden, leaders and followers, all gone under, while wretched I swim on. Yet these same reflective intervals that keep me afloat have led me into wonder, doubt, despair—strange emotions for a swimmer!—have led me, even, to suspect . . . that our night-sea journey is without meaning.

"Indeed, if I have yet to join the hosts of the suicides, it is because (fatigue apart) I find it no meaningfuller to drown myself than to go on swimming.

"I know that there are those who seem actually to enjoy the night-sea; who claim to love swimming for its own sake, or sincerely believe that 'reaching the Shore,' 'transmitting the Heritage' (*Whose* Heritage, I'd like to know? And to whom?) is worth the staggering cost. I do not. Swimming itself I find at best not actively unpleasant, more often tiresome, not infrequently a torment. Arguments from function and design don't impress me: granted that we can and do swim, that in a manner of speaking our long tails and streamlined heads are 'meant for' swimming; it by no means follows—for me, at least—that we *should* swim, or otherwise endeavor to 'fulfill our destiny.' Which is to say, Someone Else's destiny, since ours, so far as I can see, is merely to perish, one way or another, soon or late. The heartless zeal of our (departed) leaders, like the blind ambition and good cheer of my own youth, appalls me now; for the death of my comrades I am inconsolable. If the night-sea journey has justification, it is not for us swimmers ever to discover it.

"Oh, to be sure, 'Love!' one heard on every side: 'Love it is that drives and sustains us!' I translate: we don't know *what* drives and sustains us,

---

°*joie de nager:*   the joy of swimming

only that we are most miserably driven and, imperfectly, sustained. *Love* is how we call our ignorance of what whips us. 'To reach the Shore,'° then: but what if the Shore exists in the fancies of us swimmers merely, who dream it to account for the dreadful fact that we swim, have always and only swum, and continue swimming without respite (myself expected) until we die? Supposing even that there *were* a Shore—that, as a cynical companion of mine once imagined, we rise from the drowned to discover all those vulgar superstitions and exalted metaphors to be literal truth: the giant Maker of us all, the Shores of Light beyond our night-sea journey!—whatever would a swimmer do there? The fact is, when we imagine the Shore, what comes to mind is just the opposite of our condition: no more night, no more sea, no more journeying. In short, the blissful estate of the drowned.

" 'Ours not to stop and think; ours but to swim and sink. . . .' Because a moment's thought reveals the pointlessness of swimming. 'No matter,' I've heard some say, even as they gulped their last: 'The night-sea journey may be absurd, but here we swim, will-we nill-we, against the flood, onward and upward, toward a Shore that may not exist and couldn't be reached if it did.' The thoughtful swimmer's choices, then, they say, are two: give over thrashing and go under for good, or embrace the absurdity; affirm in and for itself the night-sea journey; swim on with neither motive nor destination, for the sake of swimming, and compassionate moreover with your fellow swimmer, we being all at sea and equally in the dark. I find neither course acceptable. If not even the hypothetical Shore can justify a sea-full of drownèd comrades, to speak of the swim-in-itself as somehow doing so strikes me as obscene. I continue to swim—but only because blind habit, blind instinct, blind fear of drowning are still more strong than the horror of our journey. And if an occasion I have assisted a fellow-thrasher, joined in the cheers and songs, even passed along to others strokes of genius from the drownèd great, it's that I shrink by temperament from making myself conspicuous. To paddle off in one's own direction, assert one's independent right-of-way, overrun one's fellows without compunction, or dedicate oneself entirely to pleasures and diversions without regard for conscience—I can't finally condemn those who journey in this wise; in half my moods I envy them and despise the weak vitality that keeps me from following their example. But in reasonabler moments I remind myself that it's their very freedom and self-responsibility I reject, as more dramatically absurd, in our senseless circumstances, than tailing along in conventional fashion. Suicides, rebels, affirmers of the paradox—nay-sayers and yea-sayers alike to our fatal journey—I finally shake my head at them. And splash sighing past their corpses, one by one, as past a hundred sorts of others: friends, enemies,

---

°*Shore:*   the End; in one sense, Heaven or Paradise

brothers; fools, sages, brutes—and nobodies, million upon million. I envy them all.

"A poor irony: that I, who find abhorrent and tautological° the doctrine of survival of the fittest (*fitness* meaning, in my experience, nothing more than survival-ability, a talent whose only demonstration is the fact of survival, but whose chief ingredients seem to be strength, guile, callousness), may be the sole remaining swimmer! But the doctrine is false as well as repellent: Chance drowns the worthy with the unworthy, bears up the unfit with the fit by whatever definition, and makes the night-sea journey essentially *haphazard* as well as murderous and unjustified.

" 'You only swim once.' Why bother, then?

" 'Except ye drown, ye shall not reach the Shore of Life.° Poppycock.

"One of my late companions—that same cynic with the curious fancy, among the first to drown—entertained us with odd conjectures while we waited to begin our journey. A favorite theory of his was that the Father does exist, and did indeed make us and the sea we swim—but not a-purpose or even consciously; He made us, as it were, despite Himself, as we make waves with every tail-thrash, and may be unaware of our existence. Another was that He knows we're here but doesn't care what happens to us, inasmuch as He creates (voluntarily or not) other seas and swimmers at more or less regular intervals. In bitterer moments, such as just before he drowned, my friend even supposed that our Maker wished us unmade; there was indeed a Shore, he'd argue, which could save at least some of us from drowning and toward which it was our function to struggle—but for reasons unknowable to us He wanted desperately to prevent our reaching that happy place and fulfilling our destiny. Our 'Father,' in short, was our adversary and would-be killer! No less outrageous, and offensive to traditional opinion, were the fellow's speculations on the nature of our Maker: that He might well be no swimmer Himself at all, but some sort of monstrosity, perhaps even tailless; that He might be stupid, malicious, insensible, perverse, or asleep and dreaming; that the end for which He created and launched us forth, and which we flagellate ourselves to fathom, was perhaps immoral, even obscene. Et cetera, et cetera: there was no end to the chap's conjectures, or the impoliteness of his fancy; I have reason to suspect that his early demise, whether planned by 'our Maker' or not, was expedited by certain fellow-swimmers indignant at his blasphemies.

"In other moods, however (he was as given to moods as I), his theorizing would become half-serious, so it seemed to me, especially upon the subjects of Fate and Immortality, to which our youthful conversations often turned. Then his harangues, if no less fantastical, grew solemn and obscure, and if he was still baiting us, his passion undid the joke. His objection to popular opinions of the hereafter, he would declare, was their

---

°*tautological:* redundant   °*'Except ye drown, . . . Life':*   cf. Matthew 10:39

claim to general validity. Why need believers hold that *all* the drownèd rise to be judged at journey's end, and non-believers that drowning is final without exception? In *his* opinion (so he'd vow at least), nearly everyone's fate was permanent death; indeed he took a sour pleasure in supposing that every 'Maker' made thousands of separate seas in His creative lifetime, each populated like ours with millions of swimmers, and that in almost every instance both sea and swimmers were utterly annihilated, whether accidentally or by malevolent design. (Nothing if not pluralistical, he imagined there might be millions and billions of 'Fathers,' perhaps in some 'night-sea' of their own!) However—and here he turned infidels against him with the faithful—he professed to believe that in possibly a single night-sea per thousand, say, one of its quarter-billion swimmers (that is, one swimmer in two hundred fifty billions) achieved a qualified immortality. In some cases the rate might be slightly higher; in others it was vastly lower, for just as there are swimmers of every degree of proficiency, including some who drown before the journey starts, unable to swim at all, and others created drowned, as it were, so he imagined what can only be termed impotent Creators, Makers unable to Make, as well as uncommonly fertile ones and all grades between. And it pleased him to deny any necessary relation between a Maker's productivity and His other virtues—including, even, the quality of His creatures.

"I could go on (*he* surely did) with his elaboration of these mad notions—such as that swimmers in other night-seas needn't be of our kind; that Makers themselves might belong to different *species*, so to speak; that our particular Maker mightn't Himself be immortal, or that we might be not only His emissaries but His 'immortality,' continuing His life and our own, transmogrified, beyond our individual deaths. Even this modified immortality (meaningless to me) he conceived as relative and contingent, subject to accidental or deliberate termination: his pet hypothesis was that Makers and swimmers *each generate the other*—against all odds, their number being so great—and that any given 'immortality-chain' could terminate after any number of cycles, so that what was 'immortal' (still speaking relatively) was only the cyclic process of incarnation, which itself might have a beginning and an end. Alternatively he liked to imagine cycles within cycles, either finite or infinite: for example, the 'night-sea,' as it were, in which Makers 'swam' and created night-seas and swimmers like ourselves, might be the creation of a larger Maker, Himself one of many, Who in turn et cetera. Time itself he regarded as relative to our experience, like magnitude: who knew but what, with each thrash of our tails, minuscule seas and swimmers, whole eternities, came to pass—as ours, perhaps, and our Maker's Maker's, was elapsing between the strokes of some supertail, in a slower order of time?

"Naturally I hooted with the others at this nonsense. We were young then, and had only the dimmest notion of what lay ahead; in our ignorance we imagined night-sea journeying to be a positively heroic enterprise.° Its meaning and value we never questioned; to be sure, some must go down by the way, a pity no doubt, but to win a race requires that others lose, and like all my fellows I took for granted that I would be the winner. We milled and swarmed, impatient to be off, never mind where or why, only to try our youth against the realities of night and sea; if we indulged the skeptic at all, it was as a droll, half-contemptible mascot. When he died in the initial slaughter, no one cared.

"And even now I don't subscribe to all his views—but I no longer scoff. The horror of our history has purged me of opinions, as of vanity, confidence, spirit, charity, hope, vitality, everything—except dull dread and a kind of melancholy, stunned persistence. What leads me to recall his fancies is my growing suspicion that I, of all swimmers, may be the sole survivor of this fell journey, tale-bearer° of a generation. This suspicion, together with the recent sea-change, suggests to me now that nothing is impossible, not even my late companion's wildest visions, and brings me to a certain desperate resolve, the point of my chronicling.

"Very likely I have lost my senses. The carnage at our setting out; our decimation by whirlpool, poisoned cataract, sea-convulsion; the panic stampedes, mutinies, slaughters, mass suicides; the mounting evidence that none will survive the journey—add to these anguish and fatigue; it were a miracle if sanity stayed afloat. Thus I admit, with the other possibilities, that the present sweetening and calming of the sea, and what seems to be a kind of vasty presence, song, or summons from the near upstream, may be hallucinations of disordered sensibility. . . .

"Perhaps, even, I am drowned already. Surely I was never meant for the rough-and-tumble of the swim; not impossibly I perished at the outset and have only imaged the night-sea journey from some final deep. In any case, I'm no longer young, and it is we spent old swimmers, disabused of every illusion, who are most vulnerable to dreams.

"Sometimes I think I am my drownèd friend.

"Out with it: I've begun to believe, not only that *She* exists, but that She lies not far ahead, and stills the sea, and draws me Herward! Aghast, I recollect his maddest notion: that our destination (which existed, mind, in but one night-sea out of hundreds and thousands) was no Shore, as commonly conceived, but a mysterious being, indescribable except by paradox and vaguest figure: wholly different from us swimmers, yet our complement; the death of us, yet our salvation and resurrection; simultaneously our journey's end, mid-point, and commencement; not membered and thrashing like us, but a motionless or hugely gliding sphere of unimaginable dimension; self-contained, yet dependent absolutely, in some wise, upon the chance (always monstrously improbable) that one of us will survive the night-sea journey and reach . . . Her! *Her*, he called it, or

---

°*heroic enterprise:* "progressive" views of the meaning of history °*tale-bearer:* the Artist as Survivor, as the one to tell the Generation's story

She, which is to say, Other-than-a-he. I shake my head; the thing is too preposterous; it is myself I talk to, to keep my reason in this awful darkness. There is no She! There is no You! I rave to myself; it's Death alone that hears and summons. To the drowned, all seas are calm. . . .

"Listen: my friend maintained that in every order of creation there are two sorts of creators, contrary yet complementary, one of which gives rise to seas and swimmers, the other to the Night-which-contains-the-sea and to What-waits-at-the-journey's-end: the former, in short, to destiny, the latter to destination (and both profligately, involuntarily, perhaps indifferently or unwittingly). The 'purpose' of the night-sea journey — but not necessarily of the journeyer or of either Maker! — my friend could describe only in abstractions: *consummation, transfiguration, union of contraries, transcension of categories.*° When we laughed, he would shrug and admit that he understood the business no better than we, and thought it ridiculous, dreary, possibly obscene. 'But one of you,' he'd add with his wry smile, 'may be the Hero destined to complete the night-sea journey and be one with Her. Chances are, of course, you won't make it.' He himself, he declared, was not even going to try; the whole idea repelled him; if we chose to dismiss it as an ugly fiction, so much the better for us; thrash, splash, and be merry, we were soon enough drowned. But there it was, he could not say how he knew or why he bothered to tell us, any more than he could say what would happen after She and Hero, Shore and Swimmer, 'merged identities' to become something both and neither. He quite agreed with me that if the issue of that magical union had no memory of the night-sea journey, for example, it enjoyed a poor sort of immortality; even poorer if, as he rather imagined, a swimmer-hero plus a She equaled or became merely another Maker of future night-seas and the rest, at such incredible expense of life. This being the case — he was persuaded it was — the merciful thing to do was refuse to participate; the genuine heroes, in his opinion, were the suicides, and the hero of heroes would be the swimmer who, in the very presence of the Other, refused Her proffered 'immortality' and thus put an end to at least one cycle of catastrophes.

"How we mocked him! Our moment came, we hurtled forth, pretending to glory in the adventure, thrashing, singing, cursing, strangling, rationalizing, rescuing, killing, inventing rules and stories and relationships, giving up, struggling on, but dying all, and still in darkness, until only a battered remnant was left to croak 'Onward, upward,' like a bitter echo. Then they too fell silent — victims, I can only presume, of the last frightful wave — and the moment came when I also, utterly desolate and spent, thrashed my last and gave myself over to the current, to sink or float as might be, but swim no more. Whereupon, marvelous to tell, in an instant the sea grew still! Then warmly, gently, the great tide turned,

---

°*consummation . . . categories:*   various ways of describing Romantic goals

began to bear me, as it does now, onward and upward will-I nill-I, like a flood of joy—and I recalled with dismay my dead friend's teaching.

"I am not deceived. This new emotion is Her doing; the desire that possesses me is Her bewitchment. Lucidity passes from me; in a moment I'll cry 'Love!' bury myself in Her side, and be 'transfigured.' Which is to say, I die already; this fellow transported by passion is not I; *I am he who abjures and rejects the night-sea journey!* I. . . .

"I am all love. 'Come!' She whispers, and I have no will.

"You who I may be about to become, whatever You are: with the last twitch of my real self I beg You to listen. It is *not* love that sustains me! No; though Her magic makes me burn to sing the contrary, and though I drown even now for the blasphemy, I will say truth. What has fetched me across this dreadful sea is a single hope, gift of my poor dead comrade: that You may be stronger-willed than I, and that by sheer force of concentration I may transmit to You, along with Your official Heritage, a private legacy of awful recollection and negative resolve. Mad as it may be, my dream is that some unimaginable embodiment of myself (or myself plus Her if that's how it must be) will come to find itself expressing, in however garbled or radical a translation, some reflection of these reflections. If against all odds this comes to pass, may You to whom, through whom I speak, do what I cannot: terminate this aimless, brutal business! Stop Your hearing against Her song! Hate love!

"Still alive, afloat, afire. Farewell then my penultimate hope: that one may be sunk for direst blasphemy on the very shore of the Shore. Can it be (my old friend would smile) that only utterest nay-sayers survive the night? But even that were Sense, and there is no sense, only senseless love, senseless death. Whoever echoes these refledtions: be more courageous than their author! An end to night-sea journeys! Make no more! And forswear me when I shall forswear myself, deny myself, plunge into Her who summons, singing . . .

" 'Love! Love! Love!' "

*   *   *

Although all Romantic writers are concerned with the paradoxical connections of Time, Sexuality, and Death, none concentrates so intensely on these ideas and none grasps their import more dramatically and more steadily than Dylan Thomas. Thomas writes about hardly anything else: the sense of life's inevitable movement, the contrast—bitter and sweet—between Age and Youth, between Experience and Innocence, and the paradox of the exclusively human consciousness of these facts.

DO NOT GO GENTLE INTO THAT GOOD NIGHT

Dylan Thomas (1914–1953)

Do not go gentle into that good night,
Old age should burn and rave at close of day;
Rage, rage against the dying of the light.

Though wise men at their end know dark is right,
Because their words had forked no lightning they
Do not go gentle into that good night.

Good men, the last wave by, crying how bright
Their frail deeds might have danced in a green bay,
Rage, rage against the dying of the light.

Wild men who caught and sang the sun in flight,
And learn, too late, they grieved it on its way,
Do not go gentle into that good night.

Grave men, near death, who see with blinding sight
Blind eyes could blaze like meteors and be gay,
Rage, rage against the dying of the light.

And you, my father, there on the sad height,
Curse, bless, me now with your fierce tears, I pray.
Do not go gentle into that good night.
Rage, rage against the dying of the light.

*   *   *

TWENTY-FOUR YEARS

Dylan Thomas

Twenty-four years remind the tears of my eyes.
(Bury the dead for fear that they walk to the grave in labour.)
In the groin of the natural doorway I crouched like a tailor
Sewing a shroud for a journey
By the light of the meat-eating sun.

Dressed to die, the sensual strut begun,
With my red veins full of money,
In the final direction of the elementary town
I advance for as long as forever is.

*   *   *

POEM ON HIS BIRTHDAY

Dylan Thomas

    In the mustardseed sun,
By full tilt river and switchback sea
    Where the cormorants scud,
In his house on stilts high among beaks
    And palavers of birds   5
This sandgrain day in the bent bay's grave
    He celebrates and spurns
His driftwood thirty-fifth wind turned age;
    Herons spire and spear.

    Under and round him go   10
Flounders, gulls, on their cold, dying trails,
    Doing what they are told,
Curlews aloud in the congered waves
    Work at their ways to death,
And the rhymer in the long tongued room,   15
    Who tolls his birthday bell,
Toils towards the ambush of his wounds;
    Herons, steeple stemmed, bless.

    In the thistledown fall,
He sings towards anguish; finches fly   20
    In the claw tracks of hawks
On a seizing sky; small fishes glide
    Through wynds and shells of drowned
Ship towns to pastures of otters. He
    In his slant, racking house   25
And the hewn coils of his trade perceives
    Herons walk in their shroud,

    The livelong river's robe
Of minnows wreathing around their prayer;
    And far at sea he knows,   30
Who slaves to his crouched, eternal end

Under a serpent cloud,
Dolphins dive in their turnturtle dust,
    The rippled seals streak down
To kill and their own tide daubing blood
    Slides good in the sleek mouth.

In a cavernous, swung
Wave's silence, wept white angelus knells.
    Thirty-five bells sing struck
On skull and scar where his loves lie wrecked,
    Steered by the falling stars.
And to-morrow weeps in a blind cage
    Terror will rage apart
Before chains break to a hammer flame
    And love unbolts the dark

And freely he goes lost
In the unknown, famous light of great
    And fabulous, dear God.
Dark is a way and light is a place,
    Heaven that never was
Nor will be ever is always true,
    And, in that brambled void,
Plenty as blackberries in the woods
    The dead grow for His joy.

There he might wander bare
With the spirits of the horseshoe bay
    Or the stars' seashore dead,
Marrow of eagles, the roots of whales
    And wishbones of wild geese,
With blessed, unborn God and His Ghost,
    And every soul His priest,
Gulled and chanter in young Heaven's fold
    Be at cloud quaking peace,

But dark is a long way.
He, on the earth of the night, alone
    With all the living, prays,
Who knows the rocketing wind will blow
    The bones out of the hills,
And the scythed boulders bleed, and the last
    Rage shattered waters kick
Masts and fishes to the still quick stars,
    Faithlessly unto Him

Who is the light of old
And air shaped Heaven where souls grow wild
    As horses in the foam: 75
Oh, let me midlife mourn by the shrined
    And druid herons' vows
The voyage to ruin I must run,
    Dawn ships clouted aground,
Yet, though I cry with tumbledown tongue,   80
    Count my blessings aloud:

Four elements and five
Senses, and man a spirit in love
    Tangling through this spun slime
To his nimbus bell cool kingdom come   85
    And the lost, moonshine domes,
And the sea that hides his secret selves
    Deep in its black, base bones,
Lulling of spheres in the seashell flesh,
    And this last blessing most,   90

That the closer I move
To death, one man through his sundered hulks,
    The louder the sun blooms
And the tusked, ramshackling sea exults;
    And every wave of the way   95
And gale I tackle, the whole world then,
    With more triumphant faith
Than ever was since the world was said,
    Spins its morning of praise,

I hear the bouncing hills   100
Grow larked and greener at berry brown
    Fall and the dew larks sing
Taller this thunderclap spring, and how
    More spanned with angels ride
The mansouled fiery islands! Oh,   105
    Holier then their eyes,
And my shining men no more alone
    As I sail out to die.

                    *   *   *

Dialectic

Movement may be conceptualized through the figure of dialectical opposition. This idea is central to Romantic thought and can be stated as follows: Life is a series of encounters, interactions, connections, or relations between the organism and the environment. The Self, existing as an organized whole or entity, encounters some outside stimulus, event, object, or Power that offers an antithetical or contrary experience for the self. Simply put, although living creatures have powers of self-development and energy, these powers express themselves and are to be seen when they are engaged with Otherness. As with Whitman's spider (see Part IV) the Soul can generate its own "threads," but these efforts require an "anchor," some "contrary" with which to connect.

In the usual terminology, the given condition is called a Thesis, and the outer, opposing, differentiated condition is the Antithesis. Movement, Growth, Organic Development, Motion through Time, Process, or whatever we may call it occurs when there is interaction or conflict between the given and the new. As Blake summarizes the idea: "Without Contrarities [there] is no Progression. Attraction and Repulsion, Reason and Energy, Love and Hate are necessary to Human existence."

If we imagine a human being at a given point of development or stage of maturity as a circle representing Thesis, then we may represent an outside or new experience as an arrow touching the circle at its circumference thus: $\bigcirc\leftarrow$. The process of change or growth occurs in the dialectical juxtaposition of the contrarities, creating a new entity, a new condition in which the Thesis and Antithesis are combined to form a Synthesis. This condition contains the organic and essential qualities of the old Thesis altered and developed by its encounter with the Antithesis. The Synthesis that is formed is different from either of the former two conditions, just as a child is different from either of his parents, having essential qualities of each, though changed and capable himself of new potentialities.

When the Thesis is unchallenged, when it sets up rigid barriers to the assimilation of new experience, when it is fixed, rigid, and unchanging, it fails in the primary life processes of dialectical interaction. Self-consciousness, abstraction, and forms of reason, as we have seen, tend inward, reducing the Self to abstract, alienated Categories that oppose useful organic growth involving feelings for external objects: the Mariner's water snakes, Coleridge's sympathy for Sara Hutchinson, and, in the poem that follows, Keats's sense of relationship to the figures on the urn.

The Self (the Thesis), therefore, must continue always to attempt new experience, to accept vital challenges. Like the Snout and the Night Swimmer, it must look forward to and welcome new and different things (Antitheses) as opportunities for growth and development. This energy of the Self, this Creative Will, is to Romantic metaphysics the Force that replaces the Divine Purpose of traditional thought. In Christian teleology, life is the working out of God's plan. In Romantic teleology, it is the fulfillment of as many of the individual's possibilities as possible; it is the ongoing expression of Will and Energy in meeting new opportunities.

The end of this process is, of course, death. It is the harsh fact that the Self, the Valuer of All Things, must ultimately fail, its efforts defeated by death and the extinction of consciousness, the final Antithesis that makes Romanticism a Tragic view of human experience, and shadows all mature statements of affirmative power. This tragedy, however, is not a defeat but a form of triumph, because by understanding and accepting death, the human destiny to know and experience is fulfilled.

* * *

Few poems demonstrate more brilliantly the establishment of the self in the face of the distinct and separate antithetical object and the evocation of the redemptive power of sympathy than "Ode on a Grecian Urn." The poem both tells about this process and shows it occurring. The minute changes and developments of the speaker's states of mind occur line by line, instant by instant, and should be followed and thought about carefully. They supply a detailed record of this dialectic encounter, its forms, stages, highs, and lows.

The analysis that follows the poem gives an illustrative record or reading of this development. It allows readers to see how complex and rich the thought processes of the poet are and how useful it may be to study them at this length. The same attention may profitably be given to other lyric "conversation" poems in this volume, particularly Keats' "Ode to a Nightingale" and Coleridge's "Dejection: An Ode."

ODE ON A GRECIAN URN

John Keats (1795–1821)

I

Thou still unravished bride of quietness,
　　Thou foster-child of silence and slow time,
Sylvan historian, who canst thus express
　　A flowery tale more sweetly than our rhyme:
What leaf-fringed legend haunts about thy shape　　　　5
　　Of deities or mortals, or of both,
　　　　In Tempe or the dales of Arcady?
　　What men or gods are these? What maidens loth?

What mad pursuit? What struggle to escape?
    What pipes and timbrels? What wild ecstasy?   10

II

Heard melodies are sweet, but those unheard
    Are sweeter; therefore, ye soft pipes, play on;
Not to the sensual ear, but, more endeared,
    Pipe to the spirit ditties of no tone:
Fair youth, beneath the trees, thou canst not leave   15
    Thy song, nor ever can those trees be bare;
        Bold Lover, never, never canst thou kiss.
Though winning near the goal—yet, do not grieve;
    She cannot fade, though thou hast not thy bliss,
        Forever wilt thou love and she be fair!   20

III

Ah, happy, happy boughs! that cannot shed
    Your leaves, nor ever bid the Spring adieu;
And, happy melodist, unwearièd,
    Forever piping songs forever new;
More happy love! more happy, happy love!   25
    Forever warm and still to be enjoyed,
        Forever panting, and forever young,
All breathing human passion far above,
    That leaves a heart high-sorrowful and cloyed,
        A burning forehead, and a parching tongue.   30

IV

Who are these coming to the sacrifice?
    To what green altar, O mysterious priest,
Lead'st thou that heifer lowing at the skies,
    And all her silken flanks with garlands drest?
What little town by river or sea shore,   35
    Or mountain-built with peaceful citadel,
        Is emptied of this folk, this pious morn?
And, little town, thy streets for evermore
    Will silent be; and not a soul to tell
        Why thou art desolate, can e'er return.   40

V

O Attic shape! Fair attitude! with brede
    Of marble men and maidens overwrought,

With forest branches and the trodden weed;
    Thou, silent form, dost tease us out of thought
As doth eternity: Cold Pastoral!   45
    When old age shall this generation waste,
    Thou shalt remain, in midst of other woe
Than ours, a friend to man, to whom thou say'st,
    "Beauty is truth, truth beauty,—that is all
    Ye know on earth, and all ye need to know."   50

ANALYSIS: STANZA I

Line 1:   *Thou still unravished bride of quietness,*

The urn is being addressed, and the title and situation bring the usual expectations about old Greek urns: they are old, they are in museums, and they are "classical," that is, pure and simple in line and form, a classical ideal of beauty. But interestingly, the first point that catches the poet's attention is not Pure Form, not Classical Greek Beauty, but the more amazing fact that the urn has arrived in the British Museum in 1819 without having been ravished. What ravishes most urns and most other things for that matter? Time and use destroy most urns; of the thousands of urns used by Greeks few remain intact, unravished, virginal. Moreover, the urn could be unravished only because it was married to quietness, since the usual expectation of a bride is to be ravished. One does not marry for the sake of virginity. The word "still" has two meanings: (1) yet, as in as "yet unravished," and (2) quiet, as the bride of quietness might be expected to be. In short, most things and most people are "married" to time and are ravished by time, which is noisy, not quiet. Yet ravishment is not all bad, and we see that there is a sense in which we do not wish to remain unmarried and unravished; we do not expect time to leave us alone and pure. Thus, even at the beginning the speaker presents an ambiguous sense of the urn's presence. He is impressed that it is still intact, but he is not certain that such a condition is all to the good.

Line 2:   *Thou foster-child of silence and slow time,*

Another set of epithets for the urn, parallel in construction to those of line 1. A foster-child is an orphan, one raised or taken into protection by parents but not its natural ones. The natural parents of the urn were probably either the urn maker or the culture and civilization in which the urn was designed, made, and (with the exception of this urn) used and consumed. Thus, the urn was set apart, out of its natural family; its human connection to time was broken, and like the unravished bride it is dispossessed of the natural condition of normal use. Like the bride also, there is a sense in which we may feel that to be set apart is not a happy circumstance. Orphanhood is not desirable; foster parents are a remedy for something unnatural. Quietness, silence, slow time are unusual and unnatural circumstances contrasted with the usual context in which there is action, noise, and rapid time. The speaker has yet to say any conventional things about the urn. He has not commended on its beauty, its shape, or the location of its discovery. He has ignored the little note printed by the curator which tells about the style, the composition of the clay, the date, and the wealthy family that has patronized both the archaeological dig and the museum. He has been able, in short, to avoid the conventional expressions of approval and conventional histories. He has avoided the clichés of museum-goers and preserved instead a vital, genuine response to the urn. It is here; that fact is sufficient for comment. But no judgment is possible, at least not yet. All one can say is that to be out of time is to be unlike human consciousness. The most noteworthy thing about the urn is that it is not human, and therefore it is not easy to sympathize with or to understand.

Lines 3 and 4: *Sylvan historian, who canst thus express/A flowery tale more sweetly than our rhyme!*

"Sylvan historian" means either a woodsy historian, that is, one who lives in the woods, or one who is a chronicler of woodsy things. Here the second meaning is more useful. The urn can "thus"—that is, either by being out of time and removed from human circumstances, or by means of the figures and representations on the urn's side—"express" a tale, the speaker says, more "sweetly" than poets can. The modesty of this speech should be noted because it contributes to our sense of the speaker's personality: he is self-effacing. Calling it a flowery tale, however, may be less than perfect praise, since there are other kinds of tales. A flowery tale, either ornamented, exotic, exaggerated, as in a flowery compliment, or a tale of flowers, a Romance, a story from some timeless world, may be a less valuable tale than other kinds—a plain unvarnished tale, for example. The other question raised here is exactly how a quiet urn, speaking not at all, or at least not in human words, can "express" anything. It may be said that though the speaker is going out of his way to compliment and approve the urn, he does not find that easy to do. A tale, it may be noted also, is a story occurring in time, with a beginning, middle, and end. What is the basis of an expectation that a timeless, unravished object can tell a tale, or, if a tale at all, a timeless tale?

Line 5: *What leaf-fringed legend haunts about thy shape.*

A legend is a kind of flowery tale, a tale from the past, perhaps allowing unnatural license with time and improbable events in its narrative. To be "leaf-fringed" is to be ornamented with flowery things. Perhaps in a literal sense the figures on the urn are surrounded by a motif of leafy design. Yet we notice that the legend is not "on" the urn but haunting it as, we suppose, ghosts haunt a place—that is, hang around it mistily, inhabiting it in an unnatural and inhuman sense. Normally, ghostly haunting is fearful, though here the speaker seems unafraid of the haunting. We may recall that in Greek tales, good nymphs and deities may frequent a grove or woodsy place, lending it a benign spirit. This is the first reference to the appearance of the urn. It is a plain shape, not pretty, imposing, or impressive. It is simply a shape, vague, imprecise, haunted by a vague and imprecise legend. Well, then, what legend? This is the first of many questions the speaker puts to the urn. The first four lines have addressed the urn in terms derived from the speaker's time and place, not the urn's time and place. Now he attempts to find out something of *its* point of view and the assertions of lines 1 to 4 turn to questions.

Lines 6 and 7: *Of deities or mortals, or of both, / In Tempe or the dales of Arcady?*

The speaker lacks a clear idea of the urn's meaning; he can offer only speculations about the history. A history has characters and places, but here both are vague, so vague indeed that the basic distinction between gods and human beings cannot be made. We note that Greek thought held gods and humans to be more alike than did the Judeo-Christian cultures that followed. The speaker here notes that the distinction may be incorrect: the figures may be divine *and* human. Tempe is a part of Thessaly, and Arcady is a pastoral place, a rural scene.

Line 8: *What men or gods are these? What maidens loth?*

More questions, or rather a repeated question, without answers. But no clue, no sense of who these men or gods are, or what they might tell us of their character. The maidens are new to the picture, and their state of mind is somewhat clearer. They are "loth," that is, reluctant and hesitant but not absolutely opposed. Loth to what? One of the distinctive things about Greek gods was their interest in pursuing mortal maids for sexual purposes, another point of similarity between men and gods.

Lines 9 and 10: *What mad pursuit? What struggle to escape? / What pipes and timbrels? What wild ecstasy?*

Still more questions, questions that reveal a strong human point of view, a definite human interest in love, sex, conflict, struggle, dialectic opposition between male and female. Moreover, not only are there con-flict and movement but noise: pipes, timbrels, ecstatic sounds of passion-ate erotic encounters. Such events are a long way from the peace and quiet of the bride of quietness, of the sylvan historian of pastoral scenes, with bucolic shepherds and shepherdesses tranquilly contemplating their sheep. What is the source of the noise? Clearly, the scene, the action, the definition of the protagonists, the attribution to them of any sound or motion whatever must be a function of the speaker's point of view. It must be an aspect not of the urn's quietness but of the sympathetic viewer, who can see the urn in human terms, in temporal terms, in contexts of human experience, where events occur because desire gives rise to action and movement, where sexual energy offers a primary motivation for men and maids, where experience, to use a more exalted figure, ravishes us all, ambiguously, but definitely.

A basic antithesis has been established between the pastoral quietness of the urn and the time basis of human perception. The one is quiet, simple, and pure; the other is noisy, sexy, complex, dialectic, impure, yet vigorous and vivid. The poet's sympathetic imagination has encountered an object out of context, out of time even, an object representing an ideal of shapely perfection. But this dialectic "otherness" has drawn the imagination out of the Self, and the Self has Romantically supplied a point of vision that redeems the urn from its lost timelessness. The imagination has supplied plot, character, and action and has established a connection between object and viewer, between self and other, between isolated consciousness and the world. The speaker has penetrated the object (a bride and a female shape) making it fecund, capable of life.

STANZA II

Line 11: *Heard melodies are sweet, but those unheard/Are sweeter;*

Stanza II shifts from the specific (the figures on the urn) to the general, to a summary of the questions of stanza I. This assertion acknowledges the paradoxes involved in all the imaginative efforts of stanza I. It is as if the speaker is recognizing the complaint that a reasonable person might indeed make: Where do all that music and sex come from anyway? The answer is from the imagination, that is, from a sympathetic "reading" of the data, a reading that justifies the view that a sympathetic reading makes sweeter music than a realistic, scientific, and factual reading. The latter kind is of the sort that museum curators make, but the poet's is better because it is more human, more vital, more a function of the time-filled human life as opposed to the timeless life of the urn. Yet a problem remains: Exactly what is an unheard melody? How can it exist? It is a paradox, an oxymoron, a coupling of impossible and mutually contradictory opposites. Moreover, the idea that the unreal is better than the real is Platonic. The Ideal world is better than the Real; ideals are purer, more godlike. Yet Platonic ideals worked better in geometry than in music, and Plato was suspicious of music and of poetry.

In that sense, unheard melodies are better because they are less flawed by emotion and human time consciousness. But a nagging doubt remains even as the speaker asserts this position: Can one enjoy an unheard melody? And what about other similar consequences of that view: an unseen sight, an unsmelled odor, and untasted sweet? Is the idea of the thing, unrealized, better than the thing itself? If so, then the unravished bride is better off with her Idea of Ravishment than with the fact.

Line 11: *. . . therefore, ye soft pipes, play on;*

Soft pipes have replaced the noises of the timbrels of line 10. These are the pipes of an Ideal World. The speaker asserts that they should play on, but to whom, and until when? Does an unheard melody have a coda, trio, reprise, and finale?

Lines 12 and 13: *Not to the sensual ear, but, more endeared/Pipe to the spirit ditties of no tone:*

Clearly, an unheard melody must be heard by a spiritual ear. Thus, the word "spirit" is probably best taken as a noun followed by an unseen comma. The ditties are piped to the spirit. A ditty, however, is not a symphony; it is an inconsequential tune. It is harder, therefore, to assert that unheard melodies are sweeter than heard ones because they can pipe only inconsequential tunes, tunes without tone, to the spiritual, not the real ear, and to that only softly. In another sense, however, this whole argument can be seen as an effort on the part of the speaker to give life where in effect there is none, to endow unheard, tuneless melodies with life and vitality. It is, therefore, a gallant, if necessarily unsuccessful, effort.

[This matter illustrates how careful one must be in reading the doctrinal assertions made by parts of lyrical poems. To extract this text (unheard melodies are sweeter than heard ones) and say that Keats tells us that the ideal world is better than the real world would be to ignore all the contextual qualifications and doubts surrounding that statement. Nothing in Romantic poetry is true except as a function of a particular situation—an existential truth, not an absolute one.]

Line 15: *Fair youth, beneath the trees, thou canst not leave/Thy song,*

This is the first of a series of claims made of the supposed benign consequences of the doctrine that imaginative life is better than real life. Not only is the song sweeter, but the youthful singer cannot stop singing. But again we notice that there may be doubts: to be forever engaged in singing tuneless tunes may be less than desirable.

Line 16: *. . . nor ever can those trees be bare;*

The word "leave" puts the speaker in mind of trees, though he had already noticed leaves in line 5. But a tree that cannot age, remaining forever leafy and flourishing, is another consequence of a timeless world, like unceasing song and unheard melodies. "Bare" conceals (as does its rhyme "fair") an undercurrent of a less pleasant sort. It suggests cold and winter and, distantly, time and death. Similarly, "fair" implies foul. In order to express this sympathy for the urn figures, these consequences of timelessness must not be acknowledged consciously.

Line 17: *Bold Lover, never, never canst thou kiss.*

The lovers from lines 8–10 now get attention, but they are changed from a couple to a solitary figure. A less honest speaker would have forgotten these figures. They make it more difficult than ever to argue the point that timelessness is better than timefulness, because a lover may find it even more unpleasant than singers or trees to be stuck in anticipation of the kiss yet never to know its actual consummation. Line 11 can now be rephrased to state that an unkissed kiss is better than a kissed one, or that a maid anticipating ravishment is happier than one who knows the reality. But, how bold can a lover be who has no space for action, no chance of success or failure?

Line 18: *Though winning near the goal—yet, do not grieve;*

The difficulties of asserting the argument accumulate. The speaker acknowledges that, try as he may to "defend" the urn figures, to see their condition as better than his, to see the timeless world as superior to the real world, his honesty and his true feeling force him to acknowledge the difficulties in the position he has taken. As we now see, from a human point of view, the unachieving Lover deserves not admiration but consolation and sympathy for the difficulties in his situation. "Yet, do not grieve!" What are the signs and sources of his grief? How can the speaker conclude that the lover is grieving? If he is boldly chancing a kiss, other kinds of emotion might seem more likely. But the consciousness of the speaker is human, not ideal, and that consciousness, try as it may to do otherwise, comes to human conclusions, namely, that it is better to kiss than not to kiss, that anticipation is not a sufficient substitute for consummation.

Line 19: *She cannot fade, though thou hast not thy bliss,*

This is only more consolation, as the weakness of the fundamental argument grows clearer. The fair youth cannot decline to age and ugliness, nor can she lose her vividness. That perfection, the speaker tries to argue, is compensation for the lack of bliss. "Fade" is a floral word. Flowers, leaves, and trees fade and even die though that further danger has not yet risen to the speaker's consciousness.

Line 20: *Forever wilt thou love, and she be fair!*

The absolute condition of Love is argued for as if it were to be experienced in the same static way as beauty. Beauty, one supposes, can be permanent in an urn, but not in men and women. But Love has goals, purposes, and, most importantly, acts, kisses, and consummations. It is sustained on breath, on sighs and words, and it is difficult to make the attribution of Love to the inanimate object.

STANZA III

Lines 21–22: *Ah, happy, happy boughs! that cannot shed/Your leaves, nor ever bid the Spring adieu;*

The speaker seems fixed in the same assertion as lines 11–20: that urn people, songs, maids, lovers, and even trees are better off than real people, real songs, real trees. The sterility of this argument begins to show in the flagging of the speaker's imagination. He is beginning to protest too much; he repeats the same point in the same phrases. The stronger the unconscious awareness of the problem he is avoiding becomes, the more ardently he asserts the opposite, the more he denies.

This internal dialectic, in which one part of the mind asserts one position while another part at the same time takes a contrasting position is a characteristic of the psychology of Romanticism. It reflects the sense that a mental state is not one thing but several, various responses to the given idea or situation, and that these various responses need not be similar or congruent. This poem takes its energy from the conflict between two contrasting or antithetical ideas. The poem is an account, a history, of the process by which the unconscious and truer understanding of the meaning of the urn is discovered and replaces the false condition that the conscious mind tries to assert. The speaker is trying to say that unheard melodies and permanent love are better than tunes and love in time. He is trying to assert these things not out of ignorance but out of a charitable motive, out of a wish to respond fully to the urn, to understand the meaning of the figures on it. By means of his human sympathy he is able to extend his sense of the object by showing a human understanding of the grieving lover and the boughs themselves being saved by their timelessness from the loss of leaves.

Line 23–24: *And, happy melodist, unwearièd,/Forever piping songs forever new;*

Nothing new here except that the creative, poetic speaker has a special interest in the forever-creating, never weary, never uninspired melodist. The same questions continue, however: what is the sense of the idea of "new" in a world where there is no old?

Line 25: *More happy love! more happy, happy love!*

The protests against the idea that there is something wrong with timelessness continue. Six "happy's" in five lines is not a sign of a vital and creative response. Indeed, the idea is failing, and the insipid diction displays its failure. Up to this stanza the idea, even though liable to refutation, could sustain imaginative response, could excite the speaker to feel genuinely that timelessness might indeed be a better condition. But as the language further and further betrays the failure of the assertion, we see that the speaker must see consciously what the trouble is. We may respect his sincerity, his charitable wish to protect the urn figures from the realization that they are not human, but we feel that the time has come for a better, more mature, insight.

Lines 26–27:   *Forever warm and still to be enjoyed,/Forever panting, and forever young;*
More time words applied to timelessness; warmth and breath (panting) are time functions. One cannot breathe without time and space in which to do it. And for blood to be warm it must move, circulate, animate, be refreshed with breathed oxygen. And as we have had six "happy's," we now have five "forever's."

Lines 28–30:   *All breathing human passion far above,/That leaves a heart high-sorrowful and cloyed,/A burning forehead, and a parching tongue.*
The truth tumbles out in a rush, the truth that stanza III has been trying to avoid. Perhaps the vividness of the time word "panting" makes an inescapable contrast to the artifices of the urn world. It is not, however, a pleasant truth, and we can see why the poet has gone to such lengths to avoid it. The alternative to timelessness is human time, that is, time in which consummation, depletion, sorrow, and dryness—and headache and the morning after—are consequences. Unpleasant as this is, it has the virtue of truth and knowledge. It is a step toward honesty. Better, we feel, to tell it as it is than to go on repeating happy, happy, happy.

The poem has reached a moment of new insight; the speaker has, with difficulty, told the truth. However, he has found that vision to be not particularly pleasant, and the question is whether the charitable and sympathetic spirit that has animated the poet's interest in the urn and that has now been betrayed will be lost. Will the poem turn to either despair or bitterness? How can one maintain charity and hope in the face of the facts of life, in the face of the truth of breathing human passion? The speaker's attitudes are at a crucial moment.

STANZA IV

Line 31:   *Who are these coming to the sacrifice?*
The resolution of the problem is not yet clear. We do notice, however, that the speaker's interest has returned to the urn figures to another set of representations, not lovers and maidens but a more serious procession, apparently a religious one. But the figures remain mute, and the mode of discourse between the speaker and the object remains that of questions.

Lines 32–34:   *To what green altar, O mysterious priest/Lead'st thou that heifer lowing at the skies,/And all her silken flanks with garlands drest?*
The speaker is still directing questions to the urn figures, but we notice an important difference in their quality. Now the questions put the

figures on the urn into a human time scheme, giving them a future (and in lines 35–37, a past). This seems a healthier way of dealing with the urn than to assert its Ideality and Timelessness. The speaker now imagines a new dimension: an altar, somewhere in the future and not depicted on the urn, a place that exists only on the strength of the speaker's human sense that movement has a goal, that a procession must be going to somewhere and by the same token must be coming from somewhere. The poet's imagination has turned from unsuccessful praise of the timelessness of the urn figures to an opposite strategy. If he cannot understand them by sympathetic encounters with a timeless mode, then he must try a more human mode, one that is in time and that has a past, present, and future. The dialectic established between mortals or gods (line 6) is mediated by a priest, while a heifer (a young cow, unravished) still makes another unheard noise, but an identifiable one.

Lines 35–37: *What little town by river or sea shore,/Or mountain-built with peaceful citadel,/Is emptied of this folk, this pious morn?*

The questions continue but less abstractly. The figures on the urn, having been given a destination, can also be given a history. Again, the place, the little town, is not depicted on the urn, but the speaker's imagination has now found a way to overcome the limits of that static art. He can simply treat the figures the way one treats human beings one meets, relating oneself to them by inspecting their histories. These efforts of the speaker provide a surer kind of relationship by relating the figures on the urn to life and time rather than arguing the superiority of timelessness. A better and more sympathetic state of mind on the part of the speaker is produced—and better, more substantial poetry as well. As we have seen, redemption from spiritual crisis is signaled by the ability to project one's feelings into Nature and into the personalities of others. Thus, this priest, the heifer, the altar where they go, and the little town from which they come fulfill this description of the redeemed mind.

Lines 38–40: *And, little town, thy streets for evermore/Will silent be; and not a soul to tell/Why thou art desolate, can e'er return.*

The redeemed state of mind demonstrates its powers now by extending a sympathetic response to the created objects of the imagination itself. The little town, which "exists" even less than the figures on the urn, is nonetheless given life by the speaker's sense of it, a human sense of it. It is forever empty of people and is deserving of sympathy because it is alone, having no one to speak for it. The tone here is subdued and steady, more reasonable and balanced. The speaker can find human meaning in these objects. He has escaped bitterness and the facts of reality, and he has escaped sentimentalizing as well. We can expect him to return to the larger questions, the meaning of the urn as a whole, with a clearer, *earned* sense of its worth.

Line 41:   *O Attic shape! Fair attitude!*

This line is a safe summary and a less ambitious statement than any hitherto made about the urn. It is a shape, a Greek shape, modestly fair, no longer subject to the speaker's efforts to make it into something meaningful, it stands simply and denotatively, without elaboration or grand design.

Lines 41–43:   *... with brede/Of marble men and maidens overwrought,/With forest branches and the trodden weed;*

"Brede" means embroidery or design, so that the speaker is asserting simply that the urn is a fair shape with a design of men and maidens wrought upon it. This is a cooler statement: an urn is an urn. However, a second meaning of overwrought is "overexcited," which suggests a retraction of the earlier attributions of excitement. Now that passion is seen as out of proportion, exaggerated. "Brede" also has a second meaning— "breed," as in type or species. The leaves and flowers of the tale have also changed as the speaker's perceptions improve and become more realistic. The leaves are no longer sylvan; they become branches. And the flowers become weeds, trodden down at that—realistic vision, not bitter, but cooler and accurate.

Lines 44–45:   *Thou, silent form, dost tease us out of thought/As doth eternity: Cold Pastoral!*

A still more realistic appraisal. The urn, which was said earlier to tell tales more sweetly than poetry, to give rise to unheard melodies, to portray happiness, perfection, and beauty is now seen to have none of these qualities. It is, in fact, silent, and its songs, melodies and tales were, in fact, attributes of the human imagination as the speaker looked at the urn and succeeded in constructing a relationship with it. However, the truth of the urn is none of those things that have been alleged. Indeed, the meaning the urn offers on its own without the support of the poet's sympathy is minimal. It teases but does not produce; it suggests meaning but not, ultimately, a human meaning. Its perfection and timelessness are as alien to normal human thought processes as eternity, another inhuman and intellectually sterile category. In short, the green leaves, the happy boughs, the legends, the figures, the processions, the melodies and melodists are not warm; they are indeed marble men and maids who are not passionate but cold. The urn offers not a pastoral scene but a chilling one that ultimately repels the human imagination. Perfections that do not partake of time, that portray inhuman conditions, must be seen for what they are and not be falsely pursued or confused with the realities of human experience.

Lines 46–48: *When old age shall this generation waste,/Thou shalt remain, in midst of other woe/Than ours, a friend to man, to whom thou say'st,*

But the speaker does not reject the urn. Because it is now accurately viewed, it becomes a friend to man. Because it is now seen in time, it can be accepted for the point it does make: our humanity requires that we accept the wasting of each generation, and when we can do this without bitterness, evasion, exaggeration, or resort to false identification with classical perfection, we can say that the urn remains a friend, not an evil force. Seen accurately, its "speech" can at last be heard.

Lines 49–50: *"Beauty is truth, truth beauty—that is all/Ye know on earth, and all ye need to know."*

These lines have been endlessly discussed, interpreted, and considered. Part of the problem of interpretation comes from uncertainties as to how Keats punctuated the lines. The version given here is now thought to be correct, though sometimes the quotation is closed at the middle of line 49, after the second "beauty." The confusion, however, can be resolved if we have followed the evolution of the speaker's thought from the beginning to this point and if we do not expect the poem to assert abstract doctrines but rather to speak only in context. Thus, the urn says what we might expect: from its point of view the only thing one needs to know is Beauty. Beauty and Truth, it says, however inhuman, are sufficient for life. However, the experience of the speaker shows that this view is very limited, is relative, is an assertion which the urn "means," but the meaning is not true to human experience. Urns are not, after all, alive, they are not in time, and their existence is teasing us, not producing human value. But the total experience of the speaker with the urn has been useful. He has not been led to abandon his redemptive human imagination in the face of the inhumanly beautiful, the classical perfection. He has kept his feet, as it were, on the earth, and he has worked out a human response. The poem has demonstrated the dialectic process. Confronted with an experience, an object unlike himself, the speaker takes the antithesis as a form of growth and a means of developing his consciousness.

*　　*　　*

Keats uses the same dialectic strategy in "Ode to a Nightingale" as in "Urn." In this case the bird in its unseen freedom and perfect unself-consciousness and spontaneity represents the Antithetical Idea, which contrasts to the Thesis, the depressed, isolated, and dull Self. Like other Romantic experience poems, this lyric works through the process of knowing about the nightingale, and it shows rather than tells about the process of such encounters and such means to Knowledge.

ODE TO A NIGHTINGALE

John Keats

I

My heart aches, and a drowsy numbness pains
  My sense, as though of hemlock° I had drunk,
Or emptied some dull opiate to the drains
  One minute past, and Lethe-wards° had sunk:
'Tis not through envy of thy happy lot,   5
  But being too happy in thine happiness,—
    That thou, light-wingèd Dryad° of the trees,
      In some melodious plot
  Of beechen green, and shadows numberless,
    Singest of summer in full-throated ease.   10

II

O for a draught of vintage! that hath been
  Cooled a long age in the deep-delvèd earth,
Tasting of Flora° and the country-green,
  Dance, and Provencal° song, and sunburnt mirth!
O for a beaker full of the warm South,   15
  Full of the true, the blushful Hippocrene,°
    With beaded bubbles winking at the brim,
      And purple-stainèd mouth;
  That I might drink, and leave the world unseen,
    And with thee fade away into the forest dim: 20

III

Fade far away, dissolve, and quite forget
  What thou among the leaves hast never known,
The weariness, the fever, and the fret
  Here, where men sit and hear each other groan;
Where palsy shakes a few, sad, last gray hairs,   25
  Where youth grows pale, and specter-thin, and dies;
    Where but to think is to be full of sorrow
      And leaden-eyed despairs,

°*hemlock:* a poison, the kind Socrates drank   °*Lethe:* Hades's river of forget-
fulness   °*Dryad:* wood nymph   °*Flora:* spring; Flora was the goddess of
flowers.   °*Provençal:* southern France, i.e., rural   °*Hippocrene:* The Muses's
fountain, source of poetic inspiration

Where Beauty cannot keep her lustrous eyes,
  Or new Love pine at them beyond tomorrow.   30

IV

Away! away! for I will fly to thee,
  Not charioted by Bacchus and his pards,°
But on the viewless° wings of Poesy,
  Though the dull brain perplexes and retards:
Already with thee! tender is the night,   35
  And haply the Queen-moon is on her throne,
    Clustered around by all her starry Fays;°
      But here there is no light,
  Save what from heaven is with the breezes blown
    Through verdurous glooms and winding mossy ways. 40

V

I cannot see what flowers are at my feet,
  Nor what soft incense hangs upon the boughs,
But, in embalmèd° darkness, guess each sweet
  Wherewith the seasonable month endows
The grass, the thicket, and the fruit-tree wild;   45
  White hawthorn, and the pastoral eglantine;
    Fast-fading violets covered up in leaves;
      And mid-May's eldest child,
  The coming musk-rose, full of dewy wine,
    The murmurous haunt of flies on summer eves. 50

VI

Darkling° I listen; and, for many a time
  I have been half in love with easeful Death,
Called him soft names in many a musèd rhyme,
  To take into the air my quiet breath;
Now more than ever seems it rich to die,   55
  To cease upon the midnight with no pain,
    While thou are pouring forth thy soul abroad
      In such an ecstasy!
  Still wouldst thou sing, and I have ears in vain—
    To thy high requiem become a sod. 60

°*pards:* leopards   °*viewless:* invisible   °*Fays:* fairies   °*embalmèd:* fragrant
°*Darkling:* in the dark; perhaps also a term for the bird

Thou wast not born for death, immortal Bird!
No hungry generations tread thee down;
The voice I heard this passing night was heard
In ancient days by emperor and clown:
Perhaps the self-same song that found a path   65
    Through the sad heart of Ruth,° when, sick for home,
        She stood in tears amid the alien corn;°
        The same that oft-times hath
    Charmed magic casements, opening on the foam
    Of perilous seas, in faery lands forlorn.   70

VIII

Forlorn! the very word is like a bell
To toll me back from thee to my sole self!
Adieu! the fancy° cannot cheat so well
    As she is famed to do, deceiving elf.
Adieu! adieu! thy plaintive anthem fades   75
    Past the near meadows, over the still stream,
        Up the hill-side; and now 'tis buried deep
        In the next valley-glades:
    Was it a vision, or a waking dream?
        Fled is that music:—Do I wake or sleep?   80

*   *   *

No poet worked more steadily or profoundly with Dialectic Oppositions than Yeats. His poetry is full of contrasts, oppositions, and antitheses
in dramatic dialogues, images, and symbols. These two short poems demonstrate the fundamental character of this idea. The first is a dialogue
between an old woman of dubious background and checkered career and
a bishop; the second is a simple collection of antithetical images.

°*Ruth:* **Old Testament, Book of Ruth. She accompanied her mother-in-law**
into an alien land.   °*corn:* **grain**   °*fancy:* **imagination**

CRAZY JANE TALKS WITH THE BISHOP

William Butler Yeats (1865–1939)

I MET the Bishop on the road
And much said he and I.
"Those breasts are flat and fallen now,
Those veins must soon be dry;
Live in a heavenly mansion,
Not in some foul sty."

"Fair and foul are near of kin,
And fair needs foul," I cried.
"My friends are gone, but that's a truth
Nor grave nor bed denied,
Learned in bodily lowliness
And in the heart's pride.

"A woman can be proud and stiff
When on love intent;
But Love has pitched his mansion in
The place of excrement;
For nothing can be sole or whole
That has not been rent."

THOSE IMAGES

William Butler Yeats

WHAT if I bade you leave
The cavern of the mind?
There's better exercise
In the sunlight and wind.

I never bade you go
To Moscow or to Rome.
Renounce that drudgery,
Call the Muses home.

Seek those images
That constitute the wild,
The lion and the virgin,
The harlot and the child.

Poetry is the natural language of dialectic, especially in its ability to put together logically opposing but nonetheless meaningful terms. In the following poem, the dialectical opposition between waking and sleeping, between thinking and feeling, between movement and moving, between process and goal is used to illustrate this condition.

THE WAKING

Theodore Roethke (1908–1963)

I wake to sleep, and take my waking slow.
I feel my fate in what I cannot fear.
I learn by going where I have to go.

We think by feeling. What is there to know?
I hear my being dance from ear to ear.   5
I wake to sleep, and take my waking slow.

Of those so close beside me, which are you?
God bless the Ground! I shall walk softly there,
And learn by going where I have to go.

Light takes the Tree; but who can tell us how?   10
The lowly worm climbs up a winding stair;
I wake to sleep, and take my waking slow.

Great Nature has another thing to do
To you and me; so take the lively air,
And, lovely, learn by going where to go.   15

This shaking keeps me steady. I should know.
What falls away is always. And is near.
I wake to sleep, and take my waking slow.
I learn by going where I have to go.

QUESTIONS

1. Explain the relationship between the Romantic point of view and Science.

2. What is the difference between the ways in which the Enlightenment scientist and the Romantic "knows" reality? Consider carefully the principles and logic of each position. What sort of arguments can be made on each side? Which argument is the more "modern"?

3. Why is Faust so important to Romantic thought? Discuss his story and his symbolic role for Romanticism. See the long dramatic poem by Goethe, or, for an easier version, the simpler account of Dr. Faustus by the Renaissance dramatist, Christopher Marlowe.

4. What tradition is it that failed at the end of the 18th century? What did Science have to do with the failure of that tradition? What were some of the values of the Enlightenment in which we still believe?

5. How does the Romantic make value judgments? How does he see the external world? Construct a dialogue between a Scientist and a Romantic.

6. Sincerity is the key, in Langbaum's view, to the particular form of Romantic poetry. Explain why this is so important. Which kinds of poems would carry the most sincerity? Which the least?

7. Why would one be an "admirer of the octopus"?

8. Why is Eiseley's explorer friend so alarmed about fish in the trees? Would you call Eiseley's response "alarmed"? Why or why not?

9. What were the particular characteristics of the Snout that made it the human ancestor?

10. How did these characteristics differ from those that led to insects, reptiles, and birds?

11. What does Eiseley mean when he says that the evolution of the brain allowed "laughter, or it may be sorrow" to enter in?

12. What kinds of general conditions seem to produce this change in status, this "coming ashore"? What is Romantic about the snout?

13. Why does the speaker in "Night-Sea Journey" not commit suicide?

14. Why does the speaker reject the idea of "swimming" as absurd?

15. Why does the speaker reject the idea of "paddling off in one's own direction"? Why does he not "assert one's independent right-of-way, overrun one's fellows without compunction, or dedicate oneself entirely to pleasures and diversions without regard for conscience"?

16. What is the basic difference between the speaker's points of view and those of his friends?

17. What turns out to be the Goal or End? What are the speaker's attitudes toward this Realization?

18. What are some of the activities that people use to stop time and to fix moments out of the process and movement of life? Analyze the uses

of photography, slow-motion cameras, stop-action television, instant replay, and similar electronic alterations of time.

19. What are some other places to look for symbols of the human sense of time? Consider graveyards, monuments, plaques. What do people do to assert their power over time?

20. When do we think most about time and process? What kind of experiences make us most aware of these forces? What has age got to do with it?

21. Some people speculate that the modern sense of time is different from that of the past, that the theory of the evolution of the species, the sense of the geological evolution of the earth, and the recognition of the vastness of the universe and its existence in time have altered our consciousness in a way that affects our fundamental view of ourselves. Does this seem to be a reasonable position? Discuss.

22. What attitude toward death does Dylan Thomas hold in his poems? Why is "rage" an appropriate Romantic emotion? Contrast it with other ideas about death, particularly with the current advice to accept it with equanimity and dignity.

23. Consciousness of the passage of time brings Thomas to a keener sense of the moment. The birthday is a special example of this awareness. What aspects of time and of his surroundings are most vivid to him? What are the blessings he "counts" (line 81)?

24. What aspects of redemption do these poems contain? What measure of sympathy do they contain?

25. What points of similarity and differences are to be found in a comparison of the "Nightingale" and the "Urn"?

26. The speaker in the "Nightingale" considers a number of escapes, of alternatives to his dejection. What are they and why is each one rejected?

27. What set of ideas brings the speaker to contemplate Death? What attitude does he take toward it?

28. How important is the unseen bird to the speaker's feeling? Would another Antithesis have done as well? Why or why not?

29. To what extent does the speaker succeed in generating redemptive sympathy?

30. Give additional examples to those of Crazy Jane to show that "fair needs foul."

31. In "Those Images" what is the remedy for excessive introspection.

32. What sense of time does "The Waking" suggest? What does the poem propose as a way of addressing new dialectic experiences?

33. What are the most common forms of dialectic opposition one encounters in ordinary life? What sets of opposites do we usually think of as being positively related to each other? What ones as negative in their relation? What seems to determine whether the dialectic is positive or not?

PART VI

Form

Form

All art, indeed all expression of any kind, contains oppositions between form and content, between the way the thing is being said and what is being said. A writer's or speaker's ideas are contained in words, in the language he knows, and in the laws of definition and syntax that surround him and his listener. A musician, similarly, must use notes and instruments, and a painter is constrained and supported by his canvas and his materials. This is another example of a dialectic interplay between the Romantic notion that the inner impulse be given its fullest and freest and least constrained expression and the Classical notion that emotion must be restrained, narrowed, focused, controlled, and structured.

The kind of struggle the artist has with form is influenced by both the strength and intensity of the emotional impulse and the influence of the prevailing "style" and the degree to which the style is capable of carrying the emotion. Many Romantic artists have felt the need to assert their own individuality against the restraints of the tradition. But there is danger in too great a freedom, which may produce a loss of coherence, excessive independence, and a kind of energy that may run into madness and loneliness. Perhaps in the heart of every Romantic is a yearning for the fixed disciplines of form, and in every Traditionalist a corresponding impulse to break free.

Many of Yeats's poems speak of the ways in which the form of expression of emotion consumes the emotion, and deadens the feeling. Byzantium represents a country in which the particular talent and the personality of the individual romantic artist are consumed away by a formality that touches the entire culture. But while the poet argues for the superiority of form, for its transcendence of nature and time, the world of Byzantine form is one without much life, lacking energy and process.

SAILING TO BYZANTIUM°

William Butler Yeats (1865–1939)

I

That is no country for old men. The young
In one another's arms, birds in the trees
—Those dying generations—at their song,
The salmon-falls, the mackerel-crowded seas,
Fish, flesh, or fowl, commend all summer long   5
Whatever is begotten, born, and dies.
Caught in that sensual music all neglect
Monuments of unageing intellect.

II

An aged man is but a paltry thing,
A tattered coat upon a stick, unless   10
Soul clap its hands and sing, and louder sing
For every tatter in its mortal dress,
Nor is there singing school but studying
Monuments of its own magnificence;
And therefore I have sailed the seas and come   15
To the holy city of Byzantium.

III

O sages standing in God's holy fire
As in the gold mosaic of a wall,
Come from the holy fire, perne in a gyre,°
And be the singing-masters of my soul.   20
Consume my heart away; sick with desire
And fastened to a dying animal
It knows not what it is; and gather me
Into the artifice of eternity.

°*Byzantium:* in Yeats's view a culture in which art was perfectly understood and in which the individuality of the artist was incorporated into the culture   °*perne in a gyre:* *perne* means spool and *gyre* means spiral

IV

Once out of nature I shall never take 25
My bodily form from any natural thing,
But such a form as Grecian goldsmiths make
Of hammered gold and gold enamelling
To keep a drowsy Emperor awake;
Or set upon a golden bough to sing 30
To lords and ladies of Byzantium
Of what is past, or passing, or to come.

*   *   *

Nature too reflects a dialectic play between abstract, perfection of form, and the vitalities of movement and life. Krutch speculates on this opposition in nature of form and content, between the organic vital processes of life, and the crystalline coldness of matter.

THE COLLOID AND THE CRYSTAL

Joseph Wood Krutch (1893–1970)

The first real snow was soon followed by a second. Over the radio the weatherman talked lengthily about cold masses and warm masses, about what was moving out to sea and what wasn't. Did Benjamin Franklin, I wondered, know what he was starting when it first occurred to him to trace by correspondence the course of storms? From my stationary position the most reasonable explanation seemed to be simply that winter had not quite liked the looks of the landscape as she first made it up. She was changing her sheets.

Another forty-eight hours brought one of those nights ideal for frosting the panes. When I came down to breakfast, two of the windows were almost opaque and the others were etched with graceful, fernlike sprays of ice which looked rather like the impressions left in rocks by some of the antediluvian plants, and they were almost as beautiful as anything which the living can achieve. Nothing else which has never lived looks so much as though it were actually informed with life.

I resisted, I am proud to say, the almost universal impulse to scratch my initials into one of the surfaces. The effect, I knew, would not be an

Reprinted from Joseph Wood Krutch, *The Best of Two Worlds* (New York, William Sloane Associates, 1953), pp. 143–155, by permission of the Trustees of Columbia University in the City of New York as copyright owner.

improvement. But so, of course, do those less virtuous than I. That indeed is precisely why they scratch. The impulse to mar and to destroy is as ancient and almost as nearly universal as the impulse to create. The one is an easier way than the other of demonstrating power. Why else should anyone not hungry prefer a dead rabbit to a live one? Not even those horrible Dutch painters of bloody still—or shall we say stilled?—lifes can have really believed that their subjects were more beautiful dead.

Indoors it so happened that a Christmas cactus had chosen this moment to bloom. Its lush blossoms, fuchsia-shaped but pure red rather than magenta, hung at the drooping ends of strange, thick stems and outlined themselves in blood against the glistening background of the frosty pane—jungle flower against frostflower; the warm beauty that breathes and lives and dies competing with the cold beauty that burgeons, not because it wants to, but merely because it is obeying the laws of physics which require that crystals shall take the shape they have always taken since the world began. The effect of red flower against white tracery was almost too theatrical, not quite in good taste perhaps. My eye recoiled in shock and sought through a clear area of the glass the more normal out-of-doors.

On the snow-capped summit of my bird-feeder a chickadee pecked at the new-fallen snow and swallowed a few of the flakes which serve him in lieu of the water he sometimes sadly lacks when there is nothing except ice too solid to be picked at. A downy woodpecker was hammering at a lump of suet and at the coconut full of peanut butter. One nuthatch was dining while the mate waited his—or was it her?—turn. The woodpecker announces the fact that he is a male by the bright red spot on the back of his neck, but to me, at least, the sexes of the nuthatch are indistinguishable. I shall never know whether it is the male or the female who eats first. And that is a pity. If I knew, I could say, like the Ugly Duchess, "and the moral of that is . . ."

But I soon realized that at the moment the frosted windows were what interested me most—especially the fact that there is no other natural phenomenon in which the lifeless mocks so closely the living. One might almost think that the frostflower had got the idea from the leaf and the branch if one did not know how inconceivably more ancient the first is. No wonder that enthusiastic biologists in the nineteenth century, anxious to conclude that there was no qualitative difference between life and chemical processes, tried to believe that the crystal furnished the link, that its growth was actually the same as the growth of a living organism. But excusable though the fancy was, no one, I think, believes anything of the sort today. Protoplasm is a colloid and the colloids are fundamentally different from the crystalline substances. Instead of crystallizing they jell, and life in its simplest known form is a shapeless blob of rebellious jelly rather than a crystal eternally obeying the most ancient law.

No man ever saw a dinosaur. The last of these giant reptiles was dead eons before the most dubious halfman surveyed the world about him. Not even the dinosaurs ever cast their dim eyes upon many of the still earlier creatures which preceded them. Life changes so rapidly that its later phases know nothing of those which preceded them. But the frostflower is older than the dinosaur, older than the protozoan, older no doubt than the enzyme or the ferment. Yet it is precisely what it has always been. Millions of years before there were any eyes to see it, millions of years before any life existed, it grew in its own special way, crystallized along its preordained lines of cleavage, stretched out its pseudo-branches and pseudo-leaves. It was beautiful before beauty itself existed.

We find it difficult to conceive a world except in terms of purpose, of will, or of intention. At the thought of something without beginning and presumably without end, of something which is, nevertheless, regular though blind, and organized without any end in view, the mind reels. Constituted as we are it is easier to conceive how the slime floating upon the waters might become in time Homo sapiens than it is to imagine how so complex a thing as a crystal could have always been and can always remain just what it is—complicated and perfect but without any meaning, even for itself. How can the lifeless even obey a law?

To a mathematical physicist I once confessed somewhat shame-facedly that I had never been able to understand how inanimate nature managed to follow so invariably and so promptly her own laws. If I flip a coin across a table, it will come to rest at a certain point. But before it stops at just that point, many factors must be taken into consideration. There is the question of the strength of the initial impulse, of the exact amount of resistance offered by the friction of that particular table top, and of the density of the air at the moment. It would take a physicist a long time to work out the problem and he could achieve only an approximation at that. Yet presumably the coin will stop exactly where it should. Some very rapid calculations have to be made before it can do so, and they are, presumably, always accurate.

And then, just as I was blushing at what I supposed he must regard as my folly, the mathematician came to my rescue by informing me that Laplace had been puzzled by exactly the same fact. "Nature laughs at the difficulties of integration," he remarked—and by "integration" he meant, of course, the mathematician's word for the process involved when a man solves one of the differential equations to which he has reduced the laws of motion.

When my Christmas cactus blooms so theatrically a few inches in front of the frost-covered pane, it also is obeying laws but obeying them much less rigidly and in a different way. It blooms at about Christmastime because it has got into the habit of doing so, because, one is tempted to say, it wants to. As a matter of fact it was, this year, not a Christmas cactus but a New Year's cactus, and because of this unpredictability I would like to call it "he," not "it." His flowers assume their accustomed shape and take on their accustomed color. But not as the frostflowers follow their predestined pattern. Like me, the cactus has a history which stretches back over a long past full of changes and developments. He has not always been merely obeying fixed laws. He has resisted and rebelled; he has attempted novelties, passed through many phases. Like all living things he has had a will of his own. He has made laws, not merely obeyed them.

"Life," so the platitudinarian is fond of saying, "is strange." But from our standpoint it is not really so strange as those things which have no life and yet nevertheless move in their predestined orbits and "act" though they do not "behave." At the very least one ought to say that if life is strange there is nothing about it more strange than the fact that it has its being in a universe so astonishingly shared on the one hand by "things" and on the other by "creatures," that man himself is both a "thing" which obeys the laws of chemistry or physics and a "creature" who to some extent defies them. No other contrast, certainly not the contrast between the human being and the animal, or the animal and the plant, or even the spirit and the body, is so tremendous as this contrast between what lives and what does not.

To think of the lifeless as merely inert, to make the contrast merely in terms of a negative, is to miss the real strangeness. Not the shapeless stone which seems to be merely waiting to be acted upon but the snowflake or the frostflower is the true representative of the lifeless universe as opposed to ours. They represent plainly, as the stone does not, the fixed and perfect system of organization which includes the sun and its planets, includes therefore this earth itself, but against which life has set up its seemingly puny opposition. Order and obedience are the primary characteristics of that which is not alive. The snowflake eternally obeys its one and only law: "Be thou six pointed"; the planets their one and only: "Travel thou in an ellipse." The astronomer can tell where the North Star will be ten thousand years hence; the botanist cannot tell where the dandelion will bloom tomorrow.

Life is rebellious and anarchial, always testing the supposed immutability of the rules which the nonliving changelessly accepts. Because the snowflake goes on doing as it was told, its story up to the end of time was finished when it first assumed the form which it has kept ever since. But the story of every living thing is still in the telling. It may hope and it may try. Moreover, though it may succeed or fail, it will certainly change. No form of frostflower ever became extinct. Such, if you like, is its glory. But such also is the fact which makes it alien. It may melt but it cannot die.

If I wanted to contemplate what is to me the deepest of all mysteries, I should choose as my object lesson a snowflake under a lens and an amoeba under the microscope. To a detached observer — if one can possibly imagine any observer who *could* be detached when faced with such an ultimate choice — the snowflake would certainly seem the "higher" of the two. Against its intricate glistening perfection one would have to place a shapeless, slightly turbid glob, perpetually oozing out in this direction or that but not suggesting so strongly as the snowflake does, intelligence and plan. Crystal and colloid, the chemist would call them, but what an inconceivable contrast those neutral terms imply! Like the star, the snowflake seems to declare the glory of God, while the promise of the amoeba, given only perhaps to itself, seems only contemptible. But its jelly holds, nevertheless, not only its promise but ours also, while the snowflake represents some achievement which we cannot possibly share. After the passage of billions of years, one can see and be aware of the other, but the relationship can never be reciprocal. Even after these billions of years no aggregate of colloids can be as beautiful as the crystal always was, but it can know, as the crystal cannot, what beauty is.

Even to admire too much or too exclusively the alien kind of beauty is dangerous. Much as I love and am moved by the grand, inanimate forms of nature, I am always shocked and a little frightened by those of her professed lovers to whom landscape is the most important thing, and to whom landscape is merely a matter of forms and colors. If they see or are moved by an animal or flower, it is to them merely a matter of a picturesque completion and their fellow creatures are no more than decorative details. But without some continuous awareness of the two great realms of the inanimate and the animate there can be no love of nature as I understand it, and what is worse, there must be a sort of disloyalty to our cause, to us who are colloid, not crystal. The pantheist who feels the oneness of all living things, I can understand; perhaps indeed he and I are in essential agreement. But the ultimate All is not one thing, but two. And because the alien half is in its way as proud and confident and successful as our half, its fundamental difference may not be disregarded with impunity. Of us and all we stand for, the enemy is not so much death as the not-living, or rather that great system which succeeds without ever having had the need to be alive. The frostflower is not merely a wonder; it is also a threat and a warning. How admirable, it seems to say, not living can be! What triumphs mere immutable law can achieve!

Some of Charles Peirce's° strange speculations about the possibility that "natural law" is not law at all but merely a set of habits fixed more firmly than any habits we know anything about in ourselves or in the animals suggest the possibility that the snowflake was not, after all, always inanimate, that it merely surrendered at some time impossibly remote the life which once achieved its perfect organization. Yet even if we can imagine such a thing to be true, it serves only to warn us all the more strongly against the possibility that what we call the living might in the end succumb also to the seduction of the immutably fixed.

°Charles S. Peirce (1839–1914), American philosopher

No student of the anthill has ever failed to be astonished either into admiration or horror by what is sometimes called the perfection of its society. Though even the anthill can change its ways, though even ant individuals — ridiculous as the conjunction of the two words may seem — can sometimes make choices, the perfection of the techniques, the regularity of the habits almost suggest the possibility that the insect is on its way back to inanition, that, vast as the difference still is, an anthill crytallizes somewhat as a snowflake does. But not even the anthill, nothing else indeed in the whole known universe is so perfectly planned as one of these same snowflakes. Would, then, the ultimately planned society be, like the anthill, one in which no one makes plans, any more than a snowflake does? From the cradle in which it is not really born to the grave where it is only a little deader than it always was, the ant-citizen follows a plan to the making of which he no longer contributes anything.

Perhaps we men represent the ultimate to which the rebellion, begun so long ago in some amoeba-like jelly, can go. And perhaps the inanimate is beginning the slow process of subduing us again. Certainly the psychologist and the philosopher are tending more and more to think of us as creatures who obey laws rather than as creatures of will and responsibility. We are, they say, "conditioned" by this or by that. Even the greatest heroes are studied on the assumption that they can be "accounted for" by something outside themselves. They are, it is explained, "the product of forces." All the emphasis is placed, not upon that power to resist and rebel which we were once supposed to have, but upon the "influences" which "formed us." Men are made by society, not society by men. History as well as character "obeys laws." In their view, we crystallize in obedience to some dictate from without instead of moving in conformity with something within.

And so my eye goes questioningly back to the frosted pane. While I slept the graceful pseudo-fronds crept across the glass, assuming, as life itself does, an intricate organization. "Why live," they seem to say, "when we can be beautiful, complicated, and orderly without the uncertainty and effort required of a living thing? Once we were all that was. Perhaps some day we shall be all that is. Why not join us?"

Last summer no clod or no stone would have been heard if it had asked such a question. The hundreds of things which walked and sang, the millions which crawled and twined were all having their day. What was dead seemed to exist only in order that the living might live upon it. The plants were busy turning the inorganic into green life and the animals were busy turning that green into red. When we moved, we walked mostly upon grass. Our pre-eminence was unchallenged.

On this winter day nothing seems so successful as the frostflower. It thrives on the very thing which has driven some of us indoors or underground and which has been fatal to many. It is having now its hour of triumph, as we before had ours. Like the cactus flower itself, I am a hothouse plant. Even my cats gaze dreamily out of the window at a universe which is no longer theirs.

How are we to resist, if resist we can? This house into which I have withdrawn is merely an expedient and it serves only my mere physical existence. What mental or spiritual convictions, what will to maintain to my own kind of existence can I assert? For me it is not enough merely to say, as I do say, that I shall resist the invitation to submerge myself into a crystalline society and to stop planning in order that I may be planned for. Neither is it enough to go further, as I do go, and to insist that the most important thing about a man is not that part of him which is "the product of forces" but that part, however small it may be, which enables him to become something other than what the most accomplished sociologist, working in conjunction with the most accomplished psychologist, could predict that he would be.

I need, so I am told, a faith, something outside myself to which I can be loyal. And with that I agree, in my own way. I am on what I call "our side," and I know, though vaguely, what I think that is. Wordsworth's God had his dwelling in the light of setting suns. But the God who dwells there seems to me most probably the God of the atom, the star, and the crystal. Mine, if I have one, reveals Himself in another class of phenomena. He makes the grass green and the blood red.

The following three poems reflect—the first, seriously, the second and third, humorously—on the way in which form can modify or deflect the energy or emotion of the moment.

AT A BACH CONCERT

Adrienne Rich (1929–   )

Coming by evening through the wintry city
We said that art is out of love with life.
Here we approach a love that is not pity.

This antique discipline, tenderly severe,
Renews belief in love yet masters feeling,
Asking of us a grace in what we bear.

Form is the ultimate gift that love can offer—
The vital union of necessity
With all that we desire, all that we suffer.

A too-compassionate art is half an art.   10
Only such proud restraining purity
Restores the else-betrayed, too-human heart.

THE PURIST

Ogden Nash (1903–1971)

I give you now Professor Twist,
A conscientious scientist.
Trustees exclaimed, "He never bungles!"
And sent him off to distant jungles.
Camped on a tropic riverside,
One day he missed his loving bride.
She had, the guide informed him later,
Been eaten by an alligator,
Professor Twist could not but smile.
"You mean," he said, "a crocodile."

IN PRAISE OF $(C_{10}H_9O_5)x$

John Updike (1929–   )

I have now worn the same terylene tie every day
for eighteen months.
                    —*From "Chemistry," a Penguin book by*
                              Kenneth Hutton

My tie is made of terylene;
    Eternally I wear it,
For time can never wither, stale,
    Shred, shrink, fray, fade, or tear it.
The storms of January fail   5
    To loosen it with bluster;
The rains of April fail to stain
    Its polyester lustre;
July's hot sun beats down in vain;
    October's frosts fall futilely;   10
December's snow can blow and blow—

My tie remains acutely
Immutable! When I'm below,
    Dissolving in that halcyon
Retort, my carbohydrates shed   15
    From off my frame of calcium—
When I am, in lay language, dead,
    Across my crumbling sternum
Shall lie a spanking fresh cravat
    Unsullied *ad oeternum*,   20
A grave and solemn prospect that
    Makes light of our allotted
Three score and ten, for terylene
    Shall never be unknotted.

*   *   *

QUESTIONS

1. What does Yeats find to be the primary virtue of Byzantium? Are there aspects that suggest that it is not as attractive as Yeats purports? What images in the poem suggest time and change? Which suggest fixity and permanence?
2. Explain the basic differences between the snowflake and the amoeba. What are the Classical and the Romantic characteristics of each?
3. What advantages does Adrienne Rich find in Bach? Describe the qualities of Bach's music that have this effect.

PART VII

Mockeries

Mockeries

The selections given so far offer the reader a clear idea of some of the complex ideas that comprise the large term, Romanticism. As we said at the outset, these ideas have considerable currency today, and their influence in popular culture is extensive, though most of us don't realize it.

Although it seems reasonable to admire and study authors who speak most clearly for Romantic ideas and attitudes and whose work has represented major artistic achievements of the last 200 years, the fact remains that Romantic thought has not always provided a benign or positive point of view. Like any position, intellectual or moral, it can be exaggerated, its tendencies allowed too free a rein, its excesses unchecked by a dialectic opposition.

Most of the dangers and difficulties, the psychoses and perversities, of Romantic thought derive from the emphasis on the Self, on the susceptibility to excesses in the name of Ego and Individuality. The Faust myth, with its lessons about placing personal aspirations at too high a premium or discounting too glibly the traditional values of church or state, offers a clear warning. The deification of Selfhood courts the dangers of isolation, as we have seen, but also risks other social and personal problems.

Its political consequence could be fascism. It also can breed an attitude of disdain for others, for those of less insight, less power and ability, for those of different racial or national origins. The Romantic position leads to the Self as Hero, as Mystic Leader whose mission, self-defined, becomes the creation of a unified society — the Leader (or Führer) becoming God.

This position can create personal problems as well. Defining oneself exclusively in one's own terms creates a world in which subjective reality replaces a sense of the external world, in which the Self fulfills its own needs, loses touch with the external, and falsifies experience. This may simply be a kind of insanity, a delirium that overtakes the Self and Personality when one trusts oneself too much.

Romanticism is also perhaps too greatly interested in sensation. Because feeling is first, the tendency to pursue feeling as a way of living — of placing sensation, pleasure, heightened consciousness, and exotic kinds of experience above all else — has been a part of Romantic consciousness. Romantic artists particularly have had debilitating encounters with drugs, alcohol, and sexual excesses, from Coleridge and DeQuincey down to Dylan Thomas. When this happens, the impulse to put the Self into relationships with the world is defeated. The Visionary becomes a witness only to his own inner fantasies, and the withdrawal into the occult, exoticism, and irrationality begins.

One sees the influence of these limitations in much of the popular culture of our own time, with its pursuit of pleasure as a primary aim, the tendency to subscribe to simple or anarchic political philosophies, the use of drugs to alter consciousness, and the embracing of various cults of individualism.

THE ME DECADE

Tom Wolfe (1931–   )

We are now — in the Me Decade — seeing the upward roll (and not yet the crest, by any means) of the third great religious wave in American history, one that historians will very likely term the Third Great Awakening. Like the others it has begun in a flood of *ecstasy,* achieved through LSD and other psychedelics, orgy, dancing (the New Sufi and the Hare Krishna), meditation, and psychic frenzy (the marathon encounter). This third wave has built up from more diverse and exotic sources than the first two, from therapeutic movements as well as overtly religious movements, from hippies and students of "psi phenomena" and Flying Saucerites as well as charismatic Christians. But other than that, what will historians say about it?

The historian Perry Miller credited the First Great Awakening with helping to pave the way for the American Revolution through its assault on the colonies' religious establishment and, thereby, on British colonial authority generally. The sociologist Thomas O'Dea credited the Second Great Awakening with creating the atmosphere of Christian asceticism (known as "bleak" on the East Coast) that swept through the Midwest and the West during the nineteenth century and helped make it possible to build communities in the face of great hardship. And the Third Great Awakening? Journalists (historians have not yet tackled the subject) have shown a morbid tendency to regard the various movements in this wave as "fascist." The hippie movement was often attacked as "fascist" in the late 1960s. Over the past several years a barrage of articles has attacked Scientology, the est movement, and "the Moonies" (followers of the Reverend Sun Myung Moon) along the same lines.

Frankly, this tells us nothing except that journalists bring the same conventional Grim Slide concepts to every subject. The word *fascism* derives from the old Roman symbol of power and authority, the *fasces,* a bundle of sticks bound together by thongs (with an ax head protruding from one end). One by one the sticks would be easy to break. Bound together they are invincible. Fascist ideology called for binding all classes, all levels, all elements of an entire nation together into a single organization with a single will.

The various movements of the current religious wave attempt very nearly the opposite. They begin with . . . "Let's talk about Me." They begin with the most delicious look inward; with considerable narcissism, in short. When the believers bind together into religions, it is always with a sense of splitting off from the rest of society. We, the enlightened (lit by the sparks at the apexes of our souls), hereby separate ourselves from the lost souls around us. Like all religions before them, they proselytize—but always on promising the opposite of nationalism: a City of Light that is above it all. There is no ecumenical spirit within this Third Great Awakening. If anything, there is a spirit of schism. The contempt the various seers have for one another is breathtaking. One has only to ask, say, Oscar Ichazo of Arica about Carlos Castaneda or Werner Erhard of est to learn that Castaneda is a fake and Erhard is a shallow sloganeer. It's exhilarating!—to watch the faithful split off from one another to seek ever more perfect and refined crucibles in which to fan the Divine spark . . . and to *talk about Me.*

Whatever the Third Great Awakening amounts to, for better or for worse, will have to do with this unprecedented post-World War II American development: the luxury, enjoyed by so many millions of middling folk, of dwelling upon the self. At first glance, Shirley Polykoff's slogan—"If I've only one life, let me live it as a blonde!"—seems like merely another example of a superficial and irritating rhetorical trope (*antanaclasis*) that now happens to be fashionable among advertising copywriters. But in fact the notion of "If I've only one life" challenges one of those assumptions of society that are so deep-rooted and ancient, they have no name—they are simply lived by. In this case: man's age-old belief in serial immortality.

The husband and wife who sacrifice their own ambitions and their material assets in order to provide "a better future" for their children . . . the soldier who risks his life, or perhaps consciously sacrifices it, in battle . . . the man who devotes his life to some struggle for "his people" that cannot possibly be won in his lifetime . . . people (or most of them) who buy life insurance or leave wills . . . and, for that matter, most women upon becoming pregnant for the first time . . . are people who conceive of themselves, however unconsciously, as part of a great biological stream. Just as something of their ancestors lives on in them, so will something of them live on in their children . . . or in their people, their race, their community—for childless people, too, conduct their lives and try to arrange their postmortem affairs with concern for how the great stream is going to flow on. Most people, historically, have *not* lived their lives as if thinking, "I have only one life to live." Instead they have lived as if they are living their ancestors' lives and their offspring's lives and perhaps their neighbors' lives as well. They have seen themselves as inseparable from the great tide of chromosomes of which they are created and which they pass on. The mere fact that you were only going to be here a short time and would be dead soon enough did not give you the license to try to climb out of the stream and change the natural order of things. The Chinese, in ancestor worship, have literally worshiped the great tide itself, and not any god or gods. For anyone to renounce the notion of serial immortality, in the West or the East, has been to defy what seems like a law of Nature. Hence the wicked feeling—the excitement!—of "If I've only one life, let me live it as a ————!" Fill in the blank, if you dare.

And now many dare it! In *Democracy in America,* Tocqueville (the inevitable and ubiquitous Tocqueville) saw the American sense of equality itself as disrupting the stream, which he called "time's pattern": "Not only does democracy make each man forget his ancestors, it hides his descendants from him, and divides him from his contemporaries; it continually turns him back into himself, and threatens, at last, to enclose him entirely in the solitude of his own heart." A grim prospect to the good Alexis de T.—but what did he know about . . . *Let's talk about Me!*

Tocqueville's idea of modern man lost "in the solitude of his own heart" has been brought forward into our time in such terminology as *alienation* (Marx), *anomie* (Durkheim), *the mass man* (Ortega y Gasset), and *the lonely crowd* (Riesman). The picture is always of a creature uprooted by industrialism, packed together in cities with people he doesn't know, helpless against massive economic and political shifts—in short, a creature like Charlie Chaplin in *Modern Times,* a helpless, bewildered, and dispirited slave to the machinery. This victim of modern times has always been a most appealing figure to intellectuals, artists, and architects. The poor devil so obviously needs *us* to be his Engineers of the Soul, to use a term popular in the Soviet Union in the 1920s. We will pygmalionize this sad lump of clay into a *homo novus,* a New Man, with a new philosophy, a new aesthetics, not to mention new Bauhaus housing and furniture.

But once the dreary little bastards started getting money in the 1940s, they did an astonishing thing—they took their money and ran. They did something only aristocrats (and intellectuals and artists) were supposed to do—they discovered and started doting on *Me!* They've created the greatest age of individualism in American history! All rules are broken! The prophets are out of business! Where the Third Great Awakening will lead—who can presume to say? One only knows that the great religious waves have a momentum all their own. Neither arguments nor policies nor acts of the legislature have been any match for them in the past. And this one has the mightiest, holiest roll of all, the beat that goes . . . *Me . . . Me . . . . Me . . . Me . . .*

*   *   *